MEMORANDA DURING THE WAR

The famous Matthew Brady photograph of Whitman,
taken in Washington, D.C., in 1863.

Memoranda During the War

WALT WHITMAN

Edited by Peter Coviello

OXFORD
UNIVERSITY PRESS
2004

OXFORD
UNIVERSITY PRESS

Oxford New York
Auckland   Bangkok   Buenos Aires   Cape Town   Chennai
Dar es Salaam   Delhi   Hong Kong   Istanbul   Karachi   Kolkata
Kuala Lumpur   Madrid   Melbourne   Mexico City   Mumbai   Nairobi
São Paulo   Shanghai   Taipei   Tokyo   Toronto

Published by Oxford University Press, Inc.
198 Madison Avenue
New York, New York 10016
www.oup.com

Oxford is a registered trademark of Oxford University Press

Library of Congress Cataloguing-in-Publication Data
Whitman, Walt, 1819–1892
Memoranda during the war / Walt Whitman / edited by Peter Coviello.
p. cm. Includes bibliographical references and index.
ISBN 0-19-516793-7
1. Whitman, Walt, 1819–1892—Diaries.
2. United States—History—Civil War, 1861–1865—Personal narratives.
3. United States—History—Civil War, 1861–1865—War work.
4. Poets, American—19th century—Diaries.
I. Coviello, Peter.
II. Title.
PS3231 .A355 2004
811'.3—dc22   2003022933

Illustrations throughout the book are from
the Library of Congress collections, Washington, D.C. ,
including the Manuscript Division's Feiberg–Whitman Collection (1863 notebook);
Thomas Biggs Harned Walt Whitman Collection (1862 and 1864 notebooks);
and the Rare Books Division (frontispiece)

1 3 5 7 9 0 8 6 4 2
Printed in the United States of America
on acid-free paper

CONTENTS

~ V ~

CONTENTS

Illustrations appear after page 65

ACKNOWLEDGMENTS

This edition of *Memoranda During the War* would not have been possible without the assiduous work of several generations of Whitman scholars. I would like to acknowledge in particular the work of Roy P. Basler, Kenneth M. Price, Martin G. Murray, Robert K. Nelson, and Roy Morris, Jr. For early guidance, I thank Jay Parini; for ongoing support and enthusiasm, my thanks to everyone at Oxford University Press, especially Elda Rotor. John Dorr and Alison Ferris—a librarian and curator, respectively—assisted my research in innumerable ways, material and immaterial, and they have my deepest gratitude. For their generous hospitality in Washington, D.C., I thank Larry Chernikoff, Allison Beck, and Leah Chernikoff; John Hardy, Bonnie Hardy, and Molly Hardy; Sandy Zipp (who led me to Harriet Ward Foote Hawley); and the indefatigable Karen Gliwa. For their bracing, clarifying conversation, over many months, I thank Patrick Rael and all the participants in the Bowdoin College summer "Alumni College" of 2002; Franklin Burroughs; and Alison Ferris.

INTRODUCTION

❧

Whitman at War

Our story begins with Henry James, and with one of his more notorious digressions. In 1879, in his critical biography of Nathaniel Hawthorne, James paused amid his recitations of Hawthorne's life and trials to give shape to a particular worry that, as an American novelist, he felt himself to share with the already-famed author of *The Scarlet Letter*: a worry over the airlessness, confinement, and general aridity of American national life. Describing what was for him the peculiar sensation of reading over Hawthorne's diaries of the early 1830s, James suggests that these pages have, for the fellow American, a special poignancy. "I think I am not guilty of any gross injustice in saying that the picture [the American reader] constructs from Hawthorne's American diaries, though by no means without charms of its own, is not, on the whole, an interesting one. It is characterised by an extraordinary blankness—a curious paleness of color and paucity of detail." Expanding on the notion of an American blankness, James writes himself into a veritable trance of negation. His famous catalogue of American "denudation" follows:

> The negative side of the spectacle on which Hawthorne looked out, in his contemplative saunterings and reveries, might, indeed, with a little ingenuity, be made almost ludicrous; one might enumerate the items of high civiliza-tion, as it exists in other countries, which are absent from the texture of American life, until it should become a wonder to know what was left. No State, in the European sense of the word, and indeed barely a specific national name. No sovereign, no court, no personal loyalty, no aristocracy, no church, no clergy, no army, no diplomatic service, no country gentlemen, no palaces, no castles, nor manors, nor old country-houses, nor parsonages, nor thatched cottages nor ivied ruins; no cathedrals, no abbeys, nor little Norman churches; no great Universities nor public schools—no Oxford, nor Eton, nor Harrow; no literature, no novels, no museums, no pictures, no political society, no sporting class—no Epsom nor Ascot! Some such list as that might be drawn up of the absent things in American life—especially in the American life of forty years ago, the effect of which, upon an English or a French imagination, would probably as a general thing be appalling. The natural remark, in the almost lurid light of such an indictment, would be that if these things are left out, everything is left out. The American knows that a

good deal remains; what it is that remains—that is his secret, his joke, one may say.

In terms that recall his Continental precursor Alexis de Tocqueville, James is delivered to the brink of a real despair, in *Hawthorne*, over the essentially leveling quality of American national life—a national life at once unsupported by the inheritance of centuries' worth of accumulated ritual and structure and belief, and tending, as Tocqueville observed, to valorize the blandness of equality over the glories of exceptional achievement. (As Tocqueville put it in his book *Democracy in America* [1835], "There is nothing more petty, insipid, crowded with paltry interests—in a word, antipoetic—than the daily life of an American.") Like Tocqueville, James sees in America a worrying absence of those forms of order that produce in a society not only inequality and division, but also, he suggests, grandeur, magnificence, a texture of life from which human achievements of splendor and glory are likely to emerge. What worries him is an absence, in America, of all that would be liable to produce monuments to the immensity of human striving. (For James, such monuments might have been exemplified by the gardens at Versailles, the cathedrals of Venice, the ruined palaces of a now vanished aristocracy.) The implied argument here is that hierarchy in national life, while it may indeed sponsor inequality and division and their attendant social problems, also allows for the flourishing of the truly exceptional; as such, it is a form of life whose absence James cannot help but mourn, because to him it makes unique provision for the grandeur and exaltation that are supposed to define art.

But James's sardonic look at American "society" and its prospects, eloquent and influential though it may have been, is only half right. To be sure, America was not, and could not be, Europe. For its transplanted inhabitants at least, it possessed none of the accumulated grandeur and amassed prestige of the Old World. Born as it was as a nation in a moment of decisive break from its ancestry, and unable to draw upon what one scholar calls the "massive and dense structures of inherited customary practices" that would define European nationalisms, America, and American national life, would necessarily appear blank and denuded when viewed, as in James's account, from the perspective of the looming immensity of European history and tradition. For several centuries, the comparative impoverishment of New World cultural institutions was a major theme in virtually all considerations of American national character.

Still, James's portrait of New World denudation tells an undeniably partial story of American self-understanding. There were, and there are, other stories. Had James looked back over the American experiment at an only slightly different angle, he might have seen that one of the essential elements of the American project, from the very moment of its inception, had been to seek grandeur elsewhere, and to define it otherwise. That the New World was in irreparable ways severed from the old, and located at too great a remove from its institutions and practices to be definitively stamped by them, was for many people a fact not to be mourned but, after a fashion, celebrated. For many, this great severance from the models of the past was the very key to the titanic quality of *promise* they believed to define the new American world—the very thing that made America an espe-

cially congenial environment in which to pursue dreams of reno-
vation and rebirth and self-re-creation on a scale previously
unimaginable. These dreams of a new heaven and a new earth,
of a new covenant with God, did not aspire to European structure or monumentality. Instead, they tended to make a virtue of
the comparative equality that resulted from a social order not
overly constrained by inherited hierarchy and aristocratic division. (Tocqueville begins *Democracy in America* with a note he
will return to repeatedly: "No novelty in the United States
struck me more vividly during my stay there than the equality of
conditions.") And the issue of that democratic order was, if not
anything that could properly be called political or even social
"equality," then a different but equally revolutionary ideal: the
ideal, in short, of indivisibility, of an unprecedented kind of
unity of purpose and direction among peoples distant to and
wildly disparate from one another.

Had his ear been tuned to this note, James might have gone
back as far as John Winthrop, who as he endeavored to imagine
the Puritan settlement in New England in his 1630 sermon, "A
Model of Christian Charity," as "a Citty vpon a Hill," reminded
his congregation that they would be distinguished as much by
their civic unanimity as by their piety. Of the "Covenant and
sealed... Commission" given by the Lord to the Puritans,
Winthrop says,

> wee must be knitt together in this worke as one man, wee
> must entertaine each other in brotherly Affeccion, wee
> must be willing to abridge our selues of our superfluities,
> for the suppply of others necessities, we must vphold a

familiar Commerce together in all meeknes, gentlenes, patience and liberallity, wee must delight in eache other, make others Condicions our owne reioyce together, mourne together, labour, and suffer together, allwayes haueing before our eyes our Commission and Community in the worke, our Community as members of the same body, soe shall wee keepe the vnitie of the spirit in the bond of peace.

For Winthrop, as for many following him, the singularity of American destiny was to be secured, perhaps above all else, by the unity of feeling and of purpose that could only be accomplished on this new frontier, at a saving distance from all the divisive institutions of the Old World. Here as elsewhere, the American (or in this case proto-American) claim to distinction and exalted singularity does not rest in the splendor of its institutions or in the glory of its finest citizens. But this did not mean, as James rather ruefully implied, that America was without an ideal of magnificence or exaltation. American grandeur would instead be conceived as a function of its miraculous coherence, of the deeply felt sensation of mutual belonging that, at least in the ideal, would traverse the whole of the scattered citizenry, and be available to each individual as a feeling of far-reaching connectedness, of strangely intimate attachment to the strangers who made up one's nation.

Perhaps no other writer in the American cannon better exemplifies precisely this ideal, or brings it to a higher state of articulacy, than Walt Whitman. And there is, quite certainly, no single event that tests that ideal, or Whitman's ability to imagine its fulfillment, as dramatically as the Civil War. From the moment of Whitman's appearance on July 4, 1855, in his groundbreaking volume *Leaves of Grass*—Ralph Waldo Emerson wrote from Concord to say, "I greet you at the beginning of a great career"— through the publication of expanded versions of the text in 1856 and 1860, he had made it his priority and, more accurately, his mission to secure for America an undreamt-of unanimity and coherence. As he puts it in the preface to the 1855 *Leaves of Grass*, speaking of "the United States with veins full of poetical stuff": "Their Presidents shall not be their common referee so much as their poets shall." Poetry, Whitman believed—*his* poetry—would circulate among the masses of anonymous readers and conjure among them flashes of recognition, tenderness, and affection, instilling a sensation of binding intimacy and far-flung mutual belonging. His was an ideal of nationality rooted not in the authority of the state, nor (as was increasingly common) in the racial distinction of one exalted class of Americans, but in the sense of passionate connectedness that, with the aid of his poetry, would join together even citizens as dispersed and as disparate as America's.

Whatever else it was, the Civil War marked a terrific crisis in this dream of expansive indivisibility, and not only for Whitman. One of the very finest documents of that crisis, and still one of the lesser known, is Whitman's bracing and incisive little volume *Memoranda During the War*, a book published privately, in an edition of roughly 100, in 1876, and later amended, transposed, and folded into another volume of Whitman's prose, *Specimen Days & Collect*. (Large portions of the book first appeared in a series of newspaper articles Whitman published about the war in

1874, called "'Tis But Ten Years Since.") Whitman's war experiences have long been studied and commented upon, but his brief book of prose sketches of the war has only recently begun to attract a more sustained scholarly attention, in Mark Maslan's *Whitman Possessed*, Roy Morris, Jr.'s indispensable biography of Whitman's war years, *The Better Angel*, and most especially in Robert Leigh Davis's insightful study, *Whitman and the Romance of Medicine*. (This newer work follows the lead of suggestive scholarship on Whitman and the war by such writers as Betsy Erkkila, Michael Moon, Charley Shivley, and Timothy Sweet.) Before all this, though, *Memoranda* tended to be read chiefly as a supplement, in prose, to the war poetry of *Drum-Taps* and *Memories of President Lincoln*, and one can see why. Like *Drum-Taps* and *Memories*, *Memoranda* is not a historical survey of the war, its principal players, or its great and terrible moments. One can infer the results of the bloody battles at Fredericksburg and Chancellorsville, but only because Whitman is tending to men wounded there. The finer points of strategy, the details of battle, and portraits of the most crucial military personalities, such as we find in much contemporary history, are absent here; so too are the wranglings over the political philosophy and constitutional origins of Confederate and Union claims to authority, such as we find in biographies of Lincoln or Webster or Calhoun, or in the more esoteric tomes of a contemporary of Whitman's like Confederate Vice-President Alexander Stephens. *Memoranda* is more commonly taken up, when it has been, as a revealing biographical addendum to Whitman's poetry; as a telling glimpse of the routines and culture of convalescence, in the Civil War hospitals through which so many thousands of soldiers passed; or as an intriguing, semi-private, journal-like document maintained by one of the most gifted poets of his own or any era, as he passed through a moment of profound historical upheaval.

Memoranda During the War is all these things. But it is also a story of the simultaneous deformation, and painstaking reassembly, of an idea of America. With a fervor few before him had matched, Whitman believed in an ideal of American coherence, and in the larger possibilities for human experience, both collective and individual, such an expansive mutuality would surely allow. Through the new form of his poetry, he had endeavored to imagine for the citizens of the nation a mode of belonging that compounded breadth and depth, that was at once intimately experienced—was in fact shaking in its palpable, physical intensity—and unlimited in its reach into and across the vast expanses of the republic. For such a vision of the nation, one could scarcely have imagined a more complete rebuke than the Civil War. A vivid testament to disunity, anatomization, and the indifference of citizen to distant citizen, the war seemed calculated to destroy the bluff, Emersonian optimism of a poet like Whitman. And, to some extent, the war did precisely that: especially in the postwar prose, not only of *Memoranda* but of *Democratic Vistas* as well, we find a voice vastly more tempered, more shot through with resignation and despair, than in any of Whitman's earlier work.

But *Memoranda During the War* is also a testament to the tenacity of Whitman's faith in his ideal of American coherence. The little book, with all its idiosyncrasies of form and exposition, records some of Whitman's most searching quarrels with that ideal—but not, amazingly, his abandonment of it. It is not that Whitman emerges from the war unaltered. Roy Morris Jr. reminds us that by the time the war "had claimed Lincoln," it "had also taken away a fundamental part of the poet himself, the part that believed in the blissful love of comrades as a working model for the American republic." And yet Betsy Erkkila argues that as he "tramp[ed] up and down the aisles of the hospital wards, Whitman came closer to achieving his dream of reaching the democratic masses than he would ever come through his written work." Both of them, I think, are correct. And it is precisely Whitman's often anguished ambivalence around these questions—his refusal to settle for merely comforting or merely horrifying accounts of the war—that makes *Memoranda* as fascinating, and as wrenching, as it is.

Whitman did not go to the war in search of inspiration; he went looking for his brother. In December of 1862, having read his brother's name in a casualty list from Fredericksburg, Whitman made the journey from his home in Brooklyn to Washington, D.C., from there by boat to Aquia Landing, and finally to Falmouth, Virginia, in search of any sign of George Whitman, a soldier in the 51st New York, who by the war's end had seen an immense amount of fighting, and lived to tell of it. Fearing the worst, Whitman found George alive and well and nursing an only slightly wounded cheek. (He wrote home to his mother on December 29: "When I found dear brother George, and found that he was alive and well, O you may imagine how trifling all my little cares and difficulties seemed.") There at the winter camp of the massive Army of the Potomac, he also found an entirely "new world," dense with horror and revelation: "I find deep things," he wrote to Emerson (January 17, 1863), "unrecked by current print or speech." "I now make fuller notes, or a sort of journal," he went on to say, of the "memoranda of names, items, &c" he had begun to keep at the hospitals. "This thing I will record—it belongs to the time, and to all the States—(and perhaps it belongs to me)."

Whitman had come somewhat late to the war. The first twenty months of the conflict found the poet home in New York, often in the heady bohemian company of the artists, editors, sex-radicals, and assorted intellectuals gathered in Pfaff's beer cellar, on Broadway. Out of this intoxicating milieu Whitman had written some of his most daring poetry, including the "Children of Adam" and "Calamus" clusters of *Leaves of Grass*, in the latter of which he sang "songs of manly affection" with unembarrassed openness, and preached of the politically revolutionary force of "comradeship." The impromptu field hospital set up at Lacy Mansion, looking across the Rappahannock River into Fredericksburg, was of course a radically new environment for the roustabout urban poet, and what Whitman found there rattled him out of what he called his "New York stagnation." One can, I think, exaggerate how unfamiliar and disorienting this "new world" was to Whitman, who by 1862 was in fact no stranger to horror, or for that matter to hospitals. Because of his ardent affection for the stage drivers of Manhattan—young men who enjoyed one of mid-century New York's more physically hazardous professions—Whitman had spent significant time, before the war, visiting the bedsides of injured drivers, making tours of the hospital wards, and writing of what he saw there. Still, the carnage of the Civil War hospitals was of an entirely different order. "One of the first things that met my eyes in camp," he wrote to his mother (December 29, 1862), in a passage later incorporated into *Memoranda*, "was a heap of feet, arms, legs, &c. under a tree in front of a hospital, the Lacy house."

Whitman was thus as well prepared as he could be—which is to say, only very partially prepared—for the new and august office to which he appointed himself soon after arriving in Washington. "Walt Whitman, Soldier's Missionary" he scrawled on the front cover of one of his first war notebooks. Though fanciful, this is a more accurate description of Whitman's work in the hospitals than many of those more familiarly attached to him. He was, in fact, neither nurse nor wound-dresser (though he was perfectly capable of being of assistance during any number of procedures); nor, despite an early and unsurprisingly short-lived affiliation with the Christian Commission, was Whitman in the wards to proselytize and convert, like so many of the other hospital volunteers. These were not his employments. What income he got came from working a few hours a day in the Corcoran Building as a copyist in the office of the army paymaster, Major Lyman Hapgood. (Whitman got the job through his connection to Charles W. Eldridge, a clerk in the office and a devoted friend who, along with W. W. Thayer, had published the 1860 edition of *Leaves of Grass*, and gone bankrupt doing so.) He saved on expenses—the better to pay for the gifts he distributed among the wounded—by living for much of his time in the city with the family of William D. O'Connor, a polemical novelist and abolitionist (on this point he and Whitman differed) who in a few years would defend Whitman against charges of immorality in his hagiographic work, *The Good Gray Poet*. But whatever Whitman's other involvements, his life in Washington was given structure by the hospitals and their ranks of wounded men. "I am now in and around Washington," he writes early on in *Memoranda*, "daily visiting the hospitals." There he would distribute small gifts (candies, fruit, the occasional brandy), make notes on others' needs, talk with the men, and regularly write letters home for and about them. Often he would sit in watchful silence beside soldiers too ill to speak, or nearing death. To these, too, he gave what he could: a comforting presence, promises to write to distant relatives, a hand to hold, a last kiss in this life.

These were, perhaps, humble ministrations. But they required of Whitman a great deal of emotional fortitude—a peculiar compound of tenderness and stolidity—and no small degree of physical courage. Beyond the toll taken by such proximity to the daily heartbreak of painful and untimely death, the risk of falling grievously ill through submersion in such horrifically unsanitary environments was very real. We should recall that nearly two-thirds of Civil War deaths were the result of infection and disease, and that hospitals, as well as camps, were accordingly immensely hazardous places. (Part of the tragedy of Civil War hospitals, as has often been observed, is that they operated in the last remaining years before discoveries about germs, disinfection, and sanitation revolutionized medical knowledge.) One measure of the risk to Whitman is the sharp decline of his health in the summer of 1864, requiring his removal from Washington back to Brooklyn, where he recuperated until January 1865. ("[T]his place & the hospitals seem to have got the better of me," he wrote to his mother (June 17, 1864). "I have bad nights & bad days too, some of the spells are pretty bad... the doctors have told me I must leave, that I need an entire change of air.") By early February, though, he was "back in Washington... around among the hospitals as formerly—I find quite a good many bad old lingering wounds, & also a good many down with sickness of one sort or another." Though much had changed for Whitman—most notably, his job (he now worked in the Patent Office, formerly a hospital, in the Bureau of Indian Affairs) and his health ("since I was prostrated last July, I have not had that unconscious and perfect health I formerly had")—his labors among the sick and wounded had not. Still he found himself at the bedsides of the infirm, writing letters to family on their behalf, distracting them with his gentleness and charm, doing what he could to ease and cheer them. (He would remain in Washington until 1873, when a severe stroke at last brought him back to Camden, New Jersey.) "It makes me feel quite proud," he would write to his mother (February 2, 1864), "I can do with the men what no one else at all can."

Such are some of the biographical and historical contexts, sketched in brief, of Whitman's Civil War, and one can read much of this story in the pages of *Memoranda*, which acquires more than occasionally the offhand and unstructured feel of an intermittent diary. But to read the book too credulously, to take on faith Whitman's claim that these are simply "*verbatim* renderings" of his war journals and notebooks, is to miss what we might call the achieved form of *Memoranda*, and the contest of ideas that plays out across its textual patterns and modulations. Whitman surely wished to use the work of *Memoranda* to memorialize the young men who suffered and perished in his sight, and to record as well the extraordinary life of the many hospitals he toured. But when we look more closely at its details, its rhetoric, and its figures, we see that Whitman also used the book to carry on a conversation that he had begun years before the war, and that would preoccupy him until his death.

Though they are finally volumes intended to accomplish very different kinds of memorializing work, the prose of *Memoranda* and the poetry of *Drum-Taps* do echo each other in at least one crucial respect: in both, we find a pronounced transformation in the basic rhetorical tactics Whitman had for some years been employing. These changes in Whitman's method are fascinating, in part because of how often we find them nested within several of the poet's more familiar figures and gestures. We might consider a piece from *Drum-Taps* such as "Vigil Strange I Kept on the Field One Night," a poem whose subject seems perfectly typical of Whitman, but whose treatment is in many ways a remarkable departure for him (see p. 160). In the poem, a narrator tells of his evening spent beside a wounded and dying comrade, of his tender ministrations, and of burying the boy at dawn. But this narrative emerges only rather torturously from the poem: almost every line hesitates the progression of the narrative by returning with an accretion of new modifiers to the action of a previous line. (Indeed, very little "action" happens in the poem after the first six lines.) The substance of the poem's narrative,

we soon come to discover, is actually the suspension or retarda-
tion of narrative:

> Till at latest lingering of the night, indeed just as the dawn
>   appear'd,
> My comrade I wrapt in his blanket, envelop'd well his form,
> Folded the blanket well, tucking it carefully over head and
>   carefully under feet,
> And there and then and bathed by the rising sun, my son in
>   his grave, in his rude-dug grave I deposited.

One of the things that's startling about the poem is this adamant
refusal, in its very form, to hurry the plot, to exercise any haste in
the depositing of the soldier into the earth; and the extreme formal restraint, which unfolds even at the level of the line, itself
mimes the poet's vigil and his refusal to abandon or immediately
to bury his beloved boy. Nowhere in the 1855 *Leaves of Grass*
would we find a sentence as grammatically strained as the line,
"And there and then and bathed by the rising sun, my son in his
grave, in his rude-dug grave I deposited." The syntactic reversals,
and the inclusion of one, and then another, and then another,
and still finally another modifying clause whose subject and verb
have yet to appear, repeat at the level of the line the reticence
with which the poet approaches the task of burying the boy.
Everything here must be excruciatingly delayed in its unfolding.
Not by tears or words will the poet's devotion to his comrade be
measured—"But not a tear fell, not even a long-drawn sigh,
long, long I gazed"—but by this reluctance to be parted from
him, a reluctance which the poem exercises all of its narrative

and syntactic strategies of suspension to evince. As the truncated and perfectly demotic last line attests ("And buried him where he lay"), the inhumation of the boy's body is the simplest and perhaps least crucial of the poem's events: what matters is the loving refusal to hurry to it.

The bravado and even the plain-spoken breeziness of Whitman's earlier persona—who could declare with such stark simplicity, "I am the man... I suffered... I was there"—seems here to have been stunned into a new and often wrenching tenuousness, and the world itself to have been possessed of a new and bracing recalcitrance. As in other moments in *Drum-Taps*, subjects of clauses are withheld until the very end of lines, modifiers come unglued from the words they would modify—we are offered not exactly a catalogue, nor even a sequence of contained observations, but the slow uncoiling of a narrative, in which each line executes a kind of stutter by returning to the previous line only to push forward ever so slightly at its end. Transparency of narrative and oracular immediacy are clearly not the objects here. What gets foregrounded, by contrast, is a certain recalcitrance of events with respect to their description. "Vigil Strange..." insists that there is nothing transparent about the episodes of the Civil War, least of all to the poet who would mourn its victims. The calamity of the Civil War requires of Whitman some new mode of engagement and, concomitantly, some new expressive form.

Similar transformations are on display, too, in *Memoranda*, though they operate in different registers. On the basis of *Memoranda* alone, and more certainly when his letters from the war are considered, one can fairly say that Whitman was an outrageously gifted war correspondent. (Richard Chase contends that "his style and his attitude toward what he is writing entitle Whitman to be called the first of the legendary war reporters, the literary ancestor of Ambrose Bierce, Stephen Crane, and Ernest Hemingway.") But so many of what would prove to be Whitman's most winning qualities as a writer of the war are again, from the perspective of his previous years' work, profoundly unlikely. Mutedness, restraint, delicacy, circumspection: no one would say that these qualities were absent in the pre-war editions of *Leaves of Grass*, by any means. But when those qualities did find room for themselves, they tended more often than not to be bookended by the flourishes of boisterousness, bravado, and declamatory exuberance for which Whitman is even now most famed. (There he is in the popular imagination, sounding his barbaric yawp over the roofs of the world, or unscrewing the doors from their jambs.) The reader of *Memoranda* will find moments of frenzied overstatement, to be sure, but is I think most apt to be startled by the book's mildness—or rather, by the profound reduction in volume, even as the world around the poet grows unprecedentedly loud. Though one rarely thinks of Whitman as a champion of understatement, I would say that in *Memoranda* it is the foremost device with which he presumes to manage the simultaneous immediacy and recalcitrance of the events of the war. The most crucial adverb in the book is clearly *pretty*: wounds are "pretty bad," the nights are "pretty cold," the amputation of a limb is "pretty hard." These phrases signal both intensity and stoical resignation, recognition and withholding, and embody so aptly the unsentimental fortitude that Whitman wishes to celebrate in the young men he visits.

We might think too of the muted horror of Whitman's

account, first in a letter to his mother and then transposed into *Memoranda*, of the pile of severed limbs he observed on his first day at the front: "Out doors, at the foot of a tree, within ten yards of the front of the house, I notice a heap of amputated feet, legs, arms, hands, &c., a full load for a one-horse cart." If these observations are especially chilling, it is not only because of Whitman's eye for telling detail, or the concision with which he brings into close contact the quotidian (the tree, the cart) and the ghastly. Whitman brings to the writing as well an equanimity, and a startling kind of reserve, which are strong proof against the intrusions of sententiousness and histrionic revulsion, and the failures of witness they announce. Again and again in his prose from the war, we see Whitman—an observer not typically unobtrusive—making use of a chastened idiom and a quieted self-presence to better allow the events of the war, even the most grisly or horrific, to speak for themselves. This restraint, this mildness in *Memoranda* points to a kind of humility—a recalibration of strategies in the face of a task so daunting—that is for Whitman uncharacteristic enough to be surprising and, at moments, singularly moving.

Readers of Whitman's work from before the war are liable to be moved in particular, I think, by the way these formal transformations announce not only a new method for the poet, but attest as well to what thorough devastation the war had wrought on Whitman's once-ardent utopianism, both as an American nationalist and as a poet. "The proof of a poet is that his country absorbs him as affectionately as he has absorbed it," Whitman wrote in his preface to the initial *Leaves of Grass*, and posited a crucial mutual transparency between poet and nation that the poetry of the volume would go on to corroborate: "My voice is the wife's voice," he writes in "Song of Myself," "I am an old artillerist," "I am the mashed fireman," "I am the hounded slave," and finally, conclusively: "You can do nothing and be nothing but what I will infold you." But by the time Whitman comes to write *Memoranda*, the virtually existential intimacy he posited between himself and any and all Americans has begun to fray. Consider the scene Whitman conjures as he meditates on the disastrous battle of Chancellorsville, in May of 1863:

No history ever—no poem sings, no music sounds, those bravest men of all—those deeds. No formal general's report, nor print, nor book in the library, nor column in the paper, embalms the bravest, north or south, east or west. Unnamed, unknown, remain, and still remain, the bravest soldiers. Our manliest—our boys—our hardy darlings. Indeed no picture gives them. Likely their very names are lost. Likely, the typic one of them (standing, no doubt, for hundreds, thousands,) crawls aside to some bush-clump, or ferny tuft, on receiving his death-shot— there sheltering a little while, soaking roots, grass and soil, with red blood—the battle advances, retreats, flits from the scene, sweeps by—and there, haply with pain and suffering (yet less, far less, than is supposed,) the last lethargy winds like a serpent round him—the eyes glaze in death— none recks—perhaps the burial-squads, in truce, a week afterwards, search not the secluded spot—and there, at last, the Bravest Soldier crumbles in the soil of mother earth, unburied and unknown.

The phrase "Unnamed, unknown, remain, *and still remain*," is, for Whitman, crucial. Here, the project of national history—clearly the province of Whitman's national poetry—comes up against a vision of the soldier who dies in utter solitude, to whom the nation can offer nothing in recompense, save this flattering, closely observed, yet also deeply mediated testament to his heroism. Whitman permits himself to speak here not of individual soldiers (as he does when he is at their bedsides) but of their amalgam, their condensation in a "typic one of them." Not particular, but an abstraction of particularity—a *specimen*—this soldier is visible only to the omniscient Whitman, whose avowed distance from the scene portrayed powerfully attenuates the quality of his intimacy with the dying young man. There is, finally, no knowing or becoming these soldiers, not merely because they are anonymous (anonymity is never a bar to this poet's intimacy) but because their lonely, premature deaths have excluded them from any embrace Whitman might offer, any passion for himself or for the nation he might wish to sponsor. The promise of a citizenship of impassioned intimacies cannot, finally, extend to the dead. Whitman in effect reminds us here that the messianic poet-President and his utopia of national intimacies reach their point of impossibility in the war.

There is more than this. Echoing like a refrain throughout *Memoranda* is Whitman's assertion that the "real war" will never get into the books—"Its interior history will not only never be written... [but] will never be even suggested"—a claim that, if it is backhandedly boastful (Whitman has known the war intimately enough to recognize its unique inexpressibility), also betrays a kind of authorial resignation we would never have found in his pre-war persona. The author who once claimed of the American idiom that, "It is the medium that shall well nigh express the inexpressible," in these gestures makes *all* writing— poetry, history, artful representation of whatever kind—anterior to the demands of the war and the needs of the nation. Part of what is so remarkable in this is that only a few years earlier Whitman had in effect proclaimed the reverse: that the function of poetry—his poetry—was not merely to represent the nation to itself, but to *facilitate* nationality, to sponsor the sorts of far-flung bonds between citizens of which "the nation" proper is made. His poetry, Whitman claimed, made nation-ness happen.

Consider Whitman's assertions from the preface to the 1876 *Leaves of Grass* (written as *Memoranda* was going to press), where he speaks of the devoutly nationalist, explicitly "political" purposes of his work:

> I also sent out "Leaves of Grass" to arouse and set flowing in men's and women's hearts, young and old, endless streams of living, pulsating love and friendship, directly from them to myself, now and ever. To this terrible, irrepressible yearning... this never-satisfied appetite for sympathy, and this boundless offering of sympathy—this universal democratic comradeship—this old, eternal, ever-new exchange of adhesiveness, so fitly emblematic of America—I have given in that book, undisguisedly, declaredly, the openest expression. Besides, important as they are in my purpose as emotional expressions for humanity, the special meaning of the "Calamus" cluster of "Leaves of Grass" (and more or less running through the

book, and cropping out in "Drum-Taps") mainly resides in its political significance. In my opinion, it is by a fervent, accepted development of comradeship, the beautiful and sane affection of man for man, latent in all young fellows, north and south, east and west—it is by this, I say, and by what goes directly and indirectly along with it, that the United States of the future, (I cannot too often repeat,) are to be most effectually welded together, intercalated, anneal'd into a living union.

The "Calamus" poems of 1860—in which the poet resolves to sing songs of "manly affection" and "to tell the secret of my nights and days, / To celebrate the need of comrades"—may seem at first an odd cluster for Whitman to have singled out for their "political" importance. But they become less so when we understand more precisely the idiosyncratic vision of nation cohesion into which they fit. Poems like "To a Stranger" (p. 166) and "City of Orgies" (p. 165) famously underscore the poet's amorous attentions to the city's ranks of anonymous men, his prodigious receptivity to the circuits of fascination and desire that silently crisscross the densely trafficked public spaces of the nation. (A revealing addendum to these poems of anonymous erotic exchange appears in Whitman's notebooks from the early 1860s, in which we find page after page of names: a catalogue, a litany of names, brief physical descriptions, occasional addresses or locations, and tantalizingly brief narratives.) But the cruisiness of these poems is "political" in a very specific sense. In "Whoever You Are Holding Me Now in Hand" (p. 161), Whitman articulates the matter most concisely. Here the poet imagines himself as his book—a simple enough conceit—but extends to that book all the manifold tactility, and all the flirtatious carnality, of a lover: "Or if you will, thrusting me beneath your clothing, / Where I may feel the throbs of your heart or rest upon your hip, / Carry me when you go forth over land or sea; / For thus merely touching you is enough, is best." Whitman's book does what the poet himself, in person, cannot: it circulates unendingly, not solely through his own city but even through the ranks of those whom Whitman has not and will not ever meet, into the unseen reaches of the national public (and even, as "Crossing Brooklyn Ferry" would argue, into the unseen reaches of the future). The "Calamus" poems enjoin us again and again to consider the sparks that kindle between strangers—sparks of tenderness, fascination, affection, even passion—and they do so because those bonds of passionate attachment among persons personally unknown to one another (such as the one initiated between ourselves and this flirtatious poet) simply *are* the bonds of nationality, as far as Whitman is concerned. They exemplify the anonymous intimacies of citizenship, the binding relations of Americans to their far-flung fellow Americans.

That these impassioned intimacies are most frequently wordless is also part of the point: this is not the silence of shame, or even of secrecy or a refusal to be candid, but of nimble evasion, a refusal on Whitman's part to cast such attachments in falsifying terms. These are relations, Whitman insists, that are comradely, but not chaste; filial, but not organized by ties of family; carnal, but not matrimonial. Silence, that is, is one of the ways Whitman coaxes into existence the presence of a different kind of bond, inclusive of passion but not reducible to most of the avail-

able languages of sex (which would have come back to repro-
duction and the family, sickness, or sin). And that different
bond—far-flung and anonymous but possessed as well of the
intensity of sex itself—is for Whitman the tie that, when circu-
lated across the dispersed citizenry, binds America together into
a vast and coherent collectivity. It is, accordingly, the bond his
poetry labors to incite, to propagate, and to sustain.

All of this, the war shatters. "And everywhere among these
countless graves," Whitman writes toward the end of *Memoranda*, "we see, and see, and again yet may see... the significant
word Unknown," reminding us that the dead of this war lie
beyond the affectionate embrace of the nation, and even of
memorialization. So the real war will never get in the books,
Whitman tells us, and in fact opens the volume with what is, for
him, an astounding concession: "I have perhaps forty such little
note-books left," he says of the war writings around which *Memoranda* is based,

> forming a special history of those years, *for myself alone*, full
> of associations never to be possibly said or sung. I wish I
> could convey to the reader the associations that attach to
> these soil'd and creas'd livraisons, each composed of a
> sheet or two of paper, folded small to carry in the pocket,
> and fasten'd with a pin. I leave them just as I threw them
> by during the War, blotch'd here and there with more than
> one blood-stain (emphasis added).

This is a strange and, in its way, heart-rending disclaimer from a
writer who very often registered the worth of his own works

according to the public, nationalist purposes they might successfully serve. For *Memoranda During the War*, Whitman will venture no such claims.

It is not difficult, then, to read the prose of *Memoranda* in the same vein one might read Emerson's "Experience": as a complex and self-contradicting though finally thorough recantation of previous ideals. (In this, *Memoranda* sits well beside Whitman's anguished post-war essay on American pettiness and possibility, *Democratic Vistas*.) But this is not the whole of the story of Whitman's little war book, either. For despite the real devastation of the poet's vision of national coherence that it broadcasts, the book also shows Whitman laboring quietly but determinedly, and in ingenious ways, to sustain just that vision, pushing against not only the dire circumstances of the war but against the weight of his own real ambivalences. The result of these internal tensions is a text intriguingly divided against itself—a book whose moments of nationalist ardor are consistently laced with gestures of despair and resignation, and in whose most somber memorializations we sometimes find a live current of hearty, even jubilant national pride. (Robert Leigh Davis suggestively describes this doubleness as part of a broader and deliberate method of oscillation in Whitman's war writings, a steadfast refusal to concede to the all-or-nothing Manichean logic the war seemed to engender.) The voice of nationalist idealism is not absent in *Memoranda*, but it is of a peculiar, often self-cancelling cast.

Such nationalism as we find is, for instance, often exquisitely understated, like so much of the rest of the book, and oblique in its self-proclamation. We have already noted the book's remarkable delicacy, and one of the most restrained, unsettling, and finally beautiful vignettes is "A New York Soldier," which begins rather disarmingly in the form of a newly scribbled journal entry: "This afternoon, July 22nd, I have spent a long time with Oscar F. Wilber." The passage concludes:

> He talk'd of death, and said he did not fear it. I said, "Why, Oscar, don't you think you will get well?" He said, "I may, but it is not probable." He spoke calmly of his condition. The wound was very bad, it discharg'd much. Then the diarrhoea had prostrated him, and I felt that he was even then the same as dying. He behaved very manly and affectionate. The kiss I gave him as I was about leaving he return'd fourfold. He gave me his mother's address, Mrs. Sally D. Wilber, Alleghany post-office, Cattaraugus county, N.Y. I had several such interviews with him. He died a few days after the one just described.

The final two sentences break the temporal frame of the entry: Whitman is no longer writing "this afternoon," but from the vantage of later days. The rupture is seamless enough, but Whitman's willingness to break the frame invites us to regard as all the more impressive his restraint in the passage —his capacity, in both temporal settings, to "speak calmly" as Oscar had spoken, to withhold excessive exposition or undignified keening. His must be a grief that respects Oscar's life by being both stoic and tender, "manly and affectionate"; rather like "Vigil Strange...,"

"A New York Soldier" encourages us to read the depth of Whitman's affection for the wounded as a function of his reticence in submitting their suffering to any but the most studiously reserved and matter-of-fact description. And as in so many other of Whitman's writings, not only from the war (we might think of the hounded slave passage from *Leaves of Grass*), the analogue of Christ's ministrations hovers uninsistently but clearly about the episode.

But the interest of the vignette does not end there, by any means. "A New York Soldier" is of course also revealing as an example of Whitman's unabashed amorous commerce with the nearly dead. The intensity of dignified sorrow with which he describes the deaths of individual men does not itself erase his often profound erotic attachment to them. Indeed, one has to read *Memoranda* with a deliberate obtuseness not to notice how Whitman's affections, however fraternal or avuncular or even motherly they might at moments seem, do not in any way preclude desire or carnality. Just as in "Calamus," we find all over *Memoranda* attachments that frustrate the available taxonomies of intimate relations, not least by their openness to erotic dimensions. There has been I think a good deal of misbegotten hand-wringing over these attachments, born partially of a wish not to describe anachronistically kinds of relations—desiring same-sex relations—in terms that were not current in Whitman's time. But this well-meaning hesitancy oughtn't to lead us to mantle Whitman's relations among the soldiers with a counterfeit chastity. (To do so is to forget, in the first place, the relative sexual latitude afforded to mid-century men—especially men of

middling or lower social rank—in an era before the more explicitly punishing language of sexual deviancy had gained broad cur-
rency.) The ache and passion of Whitman's imploring letters to
Lewis Brown and Thomas Sawyer, two of his most beloved soldiers, are sufficiently demonstrative, I think, to obviate any need
for what is called "harder" evidence, as is his heartbreaking letter
to the parents of Erastus Haskell (p. 168), as well as John Burroughs's cheerful account of Whitman's affection for him: "He
loves everything and everybody," Burroughs writes. "I saw a soldier the other day stop on the street and kiss him. He kisses me
as if I were a girl."

There is an uncanny similarity, too, between Whitman's infa-
mous 1860 notebooks—with their sprawling lists of names and
possible assignations—and the hospital notebooks of 1863 and
'64. These early notebooks, which compound so intriguingly a
sense of universal charity with one of a more carnal omnivorous-
ness, grade with remarkable seamlessness into the notebooks of
Whitman's war years, in which we again find list after list of
men's names, appended with small remarks on their rank, their
location, their malady, their appearance, and what was needed.
One can object that the serial assemblages of men in these notebooks provide the historian no strict corroboration of anything
in particular—which is true enough. But then we would do well
to remember that we are not, in drawing attention to the eroti-
cism of his attachments to the wounded soldiers, *accusing* the
poet of anything. To make such observations the stuff of accusa-
tion one must speak from a particular perspective, such as that of
Thomas Wentworth Higginson, who in a piece from 1882 called

"Unmanly Manhood" would accuse Whitman of wartime cow-
ardice; or of Harriet Ward Foote Hawley, nurse for the Christian Commission, who in an 1865 letter to her husband put the
matter most succinctly: "There comes that odious Walt Whitman to talk evil and unbelief to my boys. I think I would rather
see the Evil One himself—at least if he had horns and hooves… I
shall get him out as soon as possible."

We can today approach Whitman's wartime relations with a
knowingness at once more sympathetic than Hawley's and, inasmuch as we are trained by the ripe silences of "Calamus," less
narrow in its determinations than a too anachronistic perspective might prove to be. These are, again, relations that *include*
diverse dimensions, and so do not easily reduce to plainer terms;
and once we begin looking for them in *Memoranda* we start to
notice how widely, and how variously, they proliferate, marked
in almost all instances by a kind of suggestive inexplicitness.
Early on, Whitman writes:

> Besides the hospitals, I go occasionally on long tours
> through the camps, talking with the men, &c. Sometimes
> at night among the groups around the fires, in their she-
> bang enclosures of bushes. These are curious shows, full of
> characters and groups. I soon get acquainted anywhere in
> camp, with officers or men, and am always well used.

Well used…? Talking with the men, *&c.*…? These are, in themselves, unremarkable phrases—unless, of course, one has any
recollection at all of the erotic atmosphere of the "Calamus"
poems, and the suggestive withholding of information and

detail that so informs and animates them. Something of that atmosphere returns in *Memoranda*, though with a backdrop far more solemn. By virtue of these continuing feints and asides, the line one page later about the two "bright, courageous" sixteen-year-olds with amputated legs—Whitman tells us tersely: *"gave each appropriate gifts"*—can seem almost to tremble with an erotic significance whose inexplicitness is the very stuff of its charge. At times Whitman can be downright giddy about the prospect of so many men in public circulation: "Soldiers, soldiers, soldiers," he writes, "you meet everywhere in the city, often superb-looking men, though invalids dress'd in worn uniforms, and carrying canes or crutches." Yet the most arresting kind of appeal remains attached, in Whitman's eyes, to a particular kind of withholding, and many of the most resonant moments occur, again, in the intervals of silence and wordless gazing: "Then there hangs something majestic about a man who has borne his part in battles, especially if he is very quiet regarding it when you desire him to unbosom." Or again, as he writes of Thomas Haley: "Poor youth, so handsome, athletic, with profuse shining hair. One time as I sat looking at him while he lay asleep, he suddenly, without the least start, awaken'd, open'd his eyes, gave me a long, long steady look, turning his face very slightly to gaze easier—one long, clear silent look—a slight sigh—then turn'd back and went into his doze again. Little he knew, poor death-stricken boy, the heart of the stranger that hover'd near."

The figure of the soldier whose attachments, and whose very life, so exceed the language available for their description as to render him largely speechless reaches a kind of apotheosis in "Spiritual Character Among the Soldiers":

Every now and then, in hospital or camp, there are beings I meet—specimens of unworldliness, disinterestedness, and animal purity and heroism—perhaps some unconscious Indianian, or from Ohio or Tennessee—on whose birth the calmness of heaven seems to have descended, and whose gradual growing up, whatever the circumstances of work-life or change, or hardship, or small or no education that attended it, the power of a strange spiritual sweetness, fibre and inward health, have also attended. Something veil'd and abstracted is often a part of the manners of these beings. I have met them, I say, not seldom in the army, in camp, and in the hospitals. The Western regiments contain many of them. They are often young men, obeying the events and occasions about them, marching, soldiering, fighting, foraging, cooking, working on farms or at some trade before the war—unaware of their own nature, (as to that, who is aware of his own nature?) their companions only understanding that they are different from the rest, more silent, "something odd about them," and apt to go off and meditate and muse in solitude.

The critic William Aarnes is exactly right to observe that "much of this description pertains to Whitman himself." Whitman does indeed seem to share in, or at least to offer unique comprehension to, the undisplayed inner "nature" of these young men. That Whitman has encountered such sweet creatures "not seldom in the army" attests not merely to the ordinary heroism—or for that matter the serene desirability—of a young American soldiery. The passage also helps to bring into focus the recalibrated nationalism of *Memoranda*; in its wake the scattered episodes of charged intimacy and affectionate exchange between Whitman and the soldiers begin to acquire a certain gravity and coherence.

We have seen Whitman at the bedside of Stewart C. Glover, "a small and beautiful young man... very manly"; of Thomas Haley, "a fine specimen of youthful physical manliness"; by Marcus Small, for whom he wrote letters, as he did for Thomas Lindley; by Oscar Wilber, and a young Confederate soldier, "W. S. P." (William S. Prentiss), whom he "always kiss'd"; with Frank Irwin, Charles Carroll, Reuben Farwell, and scores of others. Taken together, these episodes of intimate attachment and wide-ranging circulation give shape to Whitman's undeterred nationalist resolve, inasmuch as they testify to the unforesworn presence of precisely the ideal of "Calamus"—of a national coherence secured by far-reaching bonds of affection. When we read, in "Three Years Summ'd Up," that "I made over six hundred visits and tours, and went, as I estimate, counting all, among from eighty thousand to a hundred thousand of the wounded and sick, as sustainer of spirit and body," we probably cannot be reproached for sensing in those statistics something of a boast about *circulation*, of the type a particularly self-amplifying printed author would be liable to make. In *Memoranda*, Whitman no longer circulates anonymously, in the form of his body-caressing book, but physically, in person, moving one by one through the ranks of special young American men and offering to each and to all his passionate affection. The terrible carnage of the war had made Whitman's fantasy of an enlivening, embodied circulation through print impossible: the "Calamus" project, at least as crystallized in "Whoever You Are..." founders in the Civil War, as we have seen. So Whitman resolves instead to *enact* that fantasy of self-manufactured cohesion, bed by bed, soldier by wounded soldier. (It is in this sense that critics such as Michael Moon and Betsy Erkkila see in Whitman's Civil War experiences not a cancellation but an extension of the ideals of the "Calamus" poems.) What the poet's wide-traveling book can no longer do with real or lasting effectiveness, Whitman the citizen, the "Soldier's Missionary," pledges to accomplish in person.

The degree to which Whitman both believes in this new vision, and sees in it a terrible truncation of previous ideals, is nowhere more evident than in his singular relation to Abraham Lincoln. For "August 12th," Whitman writes: "I see the President almost every day, as I happen to live where he passes to or from his lodgings out of town." Whitman's proximity to the President turns out to be more than mere happenstance, and from the detail with which he describes Lincoln's daily perambulations—where he sleeps, how he travels, at what times—we might get the impression that Whitman is, in characteristically genial fashion, tracking the President with stalker-like determination. As the astounding passage progresses, though, it becomes clear that Whitman's engagement with the President is tuned to a different note:

I see very plainly ABRAHAM LINCOLN's dark brown face, with the deep-cut lines, the eyes, always to me with a deep latent sadness in the expression. We have got so that we exchange bows, and very cordial ones... Earlier in the summer I occasionally saw the President and his wife, toward the latter part of the afternoon, out in a barouche, on a pleasure ride through the city. Mrs. Lincoln was dress'd in complete black, with a long crape veil. The equipage is of the plainest kind, only two horses, and they nothing extra. They pass'd me once very close, and I saw the President in the face fully, as they were moving slowly, and his look, though abstracted, happen'd to be directed steadily in my eye. He bow'd and smiled, but far beneath his smile I noticed well the expression I have alluded to. None of the artists or pictures has caught the deep, though subtle and indirect expression of this man's face. There is something else there. One of the great portrait painters of two or three centuries ago is needed.

Of course, Whitman has already commissioned himself as the "great portrait painter," because he alone ("always *to me*") recognizes that "deep latent sadness" in Lincoln's expression. What's extraordinary about Whitman's recognition is how perfectly it doubles the manner in which he recognizes those other, special American boys who have "something odd about them." Like them, Lincoln and his acts of affection—his bows and his eye-to-eye smiles—are marked by intense silences, and a quality of suggestive withholding that goes along with them: as Whitman tersely puts it, "There is something else there." So exactly does the "subtle and indirect" aspect of Lincoln's expression repeat the delectable opacity of personality displayed by the many young men for whom Whitman professes an inexplicit but unmistakably ardent love, that the only quasi-intimate exchanges between poet and president—they are, after all, in public—veritably shimmer with erotic portent. As Whitman stages these isolated moments, he and the president seem to share with frank flirtatiousness in the secret of each other's secret nature. They are, in all, as much like a pair of Calamus lovers passing in the street as any figures in Whitman's war writings.

At one level, the moments of communion between poet and president, and the inclusion of Lincoln among Whitman's fraternity of "special" American men, intimate a recognition of shared civic purpose between two men who endeavor, in their distinct ways, to unite the nation. Perhaps more importantly, though, Lincoln offers to Whitman a way to fulfill the broadly public, explicitly national mission he had assigned himself in the early editions of *Leaves of Grass*, but which he seemed at the outset of *Memoranda* to disclaim. The President does this, for Whitman, by standing in as a substitute, as an enfleshed synecdoche, for the bodies to which the war has made it impossible for the poet to attach himself. As we have seen, Whitman can no longer presume to extend to everyone the intimacy of his embrace, because the war has produced too great a number of irremediably unknowable American bodies. In the passage quoted above, however, he can and does profess an exciting kind of intimacy with the man in whom the very idea of the nation, in all its variousness and living disarray, is given constant unified expression. "By many has this union been help'd," Whitman writes after Lincoln's assassination, "but if one name, one man, must be pick'd out, he, most of all, is the conservator of it, to the future." Like the unknown dying soldier, Lincoln-as-President figures here as an abstraction of particularity (of the particularity of every citizen); but quite unlike the unknown soldier, Lincoln possesses as well an embodied particularity that allows Whitman's attachment to him to be of a more private, more deeply intimate nature. As he writes under the heading of "The Inauguration": "I never see that man without feeling that he is one to become personally attach'd to, for his combination of purest, heartiest tenderness, and native western form of manliness." Through this uniquely intimate and "personal" relation to the man who represents all citizens, and who as President embodies their nationness, Whitman looks to redeem the attachments blocked or forestalled by the unassimilable carnage of the war.

But if the charged, wordless intimacy with Lincoln speaks to the persistence of Whitman's unique nationalist vision, it also announces its diminishment. The very necessity of routing this redeeming affectionate embrace through a *figure* of national unity—the need to withdraw from promises of physical immediacy into the more mediated space of representation, in both of its senses—marks the concessions that were wrought from Whitman and his utopian imaginings by the war. The sometimes despairing tones of *Democratic Vistas*, his other major piece of post-war prose, are in this respect not surprising. When Whitman writes there that, "Our fundamental want to-day in the United States... is of a class, and the clear idea of a class, of native authors, literatures"; or "I submit, therefore, that the fruition of democracy, on aught like a grand scale, resides altogether in the future"; or "America has yet morally and artistically originated nothing," he is, with a stinging kind of poignancy, refusing to exonerate himself or his own labors. For the antebellum Whitman, the glorious realization of a poetic-nationalist project was a *fait accompli*: he understood *himself* to be making good, page by page and reader by reader, all those promises about the American poet and his capacities. Such is not the case in the post-war prose, where we find a tone of oblique self-reproach that is new for Whitman. In *Memoranda*, he turns to Lincoln in part because he adamantly does not wish to surrender his initial vision of American grandeur and coherence; but the need to do so, to make such use of mediated attachments and figures of symbolic authority, reminds us how wracked and circumscribed that vision had, of necessity, become.

One can argue, then, that *Memoranda* manages to remain in crucial ways a devoutly nationalist text, despite the formal qualifications that the war's many horrors precipitate, and despite Whitman's own mounting doubts and self-reproaches: it is, perhaps, a nationalism all the more arresting for the hesitations lodged within it. Even the horror of the war—which Whitman, like the doctors he admires, is determined to view with "generally impassive indifference"—accrues about it a kind of nationalistic splendor. Whitman relates without censure the cruelties of both sides, the torture and dismemberment of men, and the ruthlessness with which even the crawling wounded are picked off from afar by gunmen, because these events, taken together, attest in their very monstrosity to the unsurpassed grandeur of the nation. "[N]ever one more desperate in any age of land," he would write of the contest boiling over the nation, thereby equating the terribleness of this national war with the exemplarity, among nations, of America. By unleashing horrors so acute, so previously unimaginable, America, in Whitman's view, has finally and materially accomplished the vastness of itself. "It may have been odd," he writes as he observes column after column of soldiers trudging toward "the extreme front" in the Virginia night, "but I never before so realized the majesty and reality of the American people *en masse*. It fell upon me like a great awe." That such majesty is bound up in the practice of human slaughter neither escapes Whitman nor fazes him. A fairly morbid species of nationalism thus animates *Memoranda*, and it is realized in the often celebratory portrait of a heroic America, supremest of nations if only for having wrought upon itself a devastation far surpassing any the world had ever seen.

But this is, again, a nationalism severely qualified. The Civil War unravels the transparency of poet and nation to one another by producing, in numbers unassimilably vast, unknown and impossible to recognize American corpses. These dead, Whitman insists, cannot be imagined as merely incidental to the nation, because each has given over to the nation a body, a person, a whole cosmos of possibility, for which it can provide no recompense. Whitman's utopian poetic nationalism—its promise of a citizenship of passionate intimacies—dies with those many thousands of soldiers whose graves are marked "Unknown." Whatever national authority Whitman's poetic persona had accrued to itself, by promising an intimate embrace to all the nation's anonymous citizens, seems also to have been exhausted by the war; as *Democratic Vistas* argues, after the war new forms would have to develop, and with them a new class of authors and literatures. *Memoranda During the War*, with its unknown soldiers and scenes of tender, passionate exchange, with soldiers as well as Presidents, stands as one of Whitman's great post-war attempts to find replenishment for a badly tattered vision of American possibility.

*   *   *

It is tempting to leave matters here, with a sense of Whitman as another kind of war hero: a man who saw his vision of the nation and its grand potentialities laid waste by the carnage of war, but who would not relinquish it, and labored instead against dread and illness and loss to preserve for a more hospitable future some semblance of an earlier dream. If, like Joshua Lawrence Chamberlain or Clara Barton or General Lee or Lincoln himself, Whitman too is a hero of the war—and I think he is—it is because of this straining refusal to see wholly extinguished an idea of America, even if it means turning what had been the stuff of imagination into daily, physical, self-endangering practice. The document of that particular brand of heroism is *Memoranda During the War*.

But hero stories are almost always myths, involved not minimally with various acts of distortion and amnesia. *Memoranda* is, as we noted, pieced together largely from articles published in the New York *Weekly Graphic* in the winter of 1874, entered into copyright in 1875, and published finally in 1876, to go along with Whitman's special "Centennial Edition" of *Leaves of Grass*. As such, the book was intended, as critics have observed, as a reminder, to a nation that seemed all too liable to forget, of the astounding bravery, suffering, and loss of a war only a decade past. By the time *Memoranda* appeared, though, such memorializing impulses—and more specifically the languages of the war's recollection—were difficult to separate from altogether more complicated, less benign political motives.

Eighteen-seventy-six was one of the ugliest years in American history. The nation had lived through a violent cataclysm, only then to bear witness to a sham presidential election; unchecked displacement and slaughter of native peoples across the West; the beginnings of a truly massive agglomeration of capital in the hands of an empowered and emboldened few; and behind and beneath all this, a catastrophe in the South, sanctioned by the North: the collapse of Reconstruction, and with it the steady revocation from newly liberated black America of virtually all the securities, freedoms, and privileges the end of the war had promised. Whitman's book both glimpses these things—he speaks at the outset of "the mushy influences of current times"— and, unwittingly or otherwise, joins in the chorus of voices papering them over with tributes to by-gone heroism and celebrations of a unified nation, miraculously preserved. The brief account he gives of "the measureless degradation and insult" of Reconstruction—"the black domination, but little above beasts"—does little to assuage one's fear that in his exultant sense of a union rejoined Whitman dramatically underplays the war's great failure: to secure for *all* Americans a just and equal freedom. He knows well enough that the matter is still before the nation: "Did the vast mass of the blacks, in Slavery in the United States, present a terrible and deeply complicated problem through the just ending century?" he writes perceptively toward the end of *Memoranda*. "But how if the mass of the blacks in freedom in the U.S. all through the ensuing century, should present a more terrible and more deeply complicated problem?" If there is an admirable charity and refusal of triumphalism in his deference to the South, and his assertion that "out of the War, after all, *they* have gained a more substantial victory than anybody," there is also the dismaying sense that Whitman, too, was not unwilling to see true black freedom sacrificed in the name of a more fully mended breach between North and South. Here as virtually everywhere for Whitman, the cause of American unanimity and coherence is uppermost, whatever its cost.

Intriguingly, though, Whitman does not take up a story of national self-conception that was easily available to him—or, at least, he does not do so often. The notion of an America unified above all else by loss, its citizens knit together not by region or race or caste but by a quality of grief that traverses them all equally, was no less compelling in Whitman's time than it is, perhaps all the more spectacularly so, in our own. We might read back a not at all untypical *New York Times* headline from September of 2002—"A Single Grief Knits Together a Vast Country"—and wonder how Whitman, a century-and-a-half earlier, could have resisted such a notion after the war. For here is a way of imagining the nation that translates an inner or private experience of suffering, loss, or grief into a mode of intimate connection with the vast numbers of anonymous others who are understood to share in that bereavement, to feel it in simultaneity. This is not, finally, a style of nationalist imagining Whitman chooses to adopt in *Memoranda*, perhaps because it verges too closely on the kind of "sentimentalism" he both disparaged and flirted with throughout his work. But as his writings on the assassination and death of his beloved President Lincoln make evident, neither the appeal nor the relevance of such a model of coherence was lost on him:

The final use of the greatest men of a Nation is, after all, not with reference to their deeds in themselves, or their direct bearing on their times or lands. The final use of a heroic-eminent life—and especially a heroic-eminent death—is its indirect filtering into the nation and the race... Then there is a cement to the whole people, subtler, more underlying, than any thing in written constitution, or courts or armies—namely, the cement of a death identi-fied thoroughly with that people, at its head, and for its sake. Strange, (is it not?) that battles, martyrs, agonies, blood, even assassination, should so condense—perhaps only really, lastingly condense—a Nationality.

Here in the new millennium, these words speak to us with a chilling prescience: Whitman articulates quite concisely what is, today, the very grammar and syntax of American nationality in the post-9/11 world. But *Memoranda* is perhaps just as telling for its refusal to adapt itself wholly to any ideal of national coher-ence rooted principally in our mortal susceptibility to grief, wounding, and loss—a refusal we might wish to consider, here in our own dark times. *Memoranda During the War* does indeed address itself to the lacerations of loss and death, and does so with an aching clarity; but for all that articulacy, I think it speaks even more eloquently to a slightly different kind of anguish. The book is a testament to one man's struggle to sustain his belief in the better possibilities of American life, even as the best of his countrymen set about butchering one another, and, later, as politicians—guardians of the public good—ransacked the insti-tutions of governance with a frightening avariciousness. Until

1861, Whitman's was a largely untempered faith in the limitless possibilities of an American cohesion made of comradeship and the bonds of sane affection; during the war this faith was at once—and often in the selfsame gesture—demolished and replenished, repudiated and born anew. The immense effort of imagination Whitman displays for us in *Memoranda*—the effort to nourish an idea of America in and through the catastrophe of its present and recent past—is instructive. We have no less need today for what is found there.

Selected Bibliography

Aarnes, William. "'Free Margins': Identity and Silence in Whitman's *Specimen Days.*" *ESQ* 28:4 (1982), 243–260.

Aaron, Daniel. *The Unwritten War: American Writers and the Civil War.* New York: Knopf, 1973.

Chase, Richard. *Walt Whitman Reconsidered.* New York: William Sloane, 1955.

Coviello, Peter. "Intimate Nationality: Anonymity and Attachment in Whitman." *American Literature* 73:1 (2001), 85–119.

Davis, Robert Leigh. *Whitman and the Romance of Medicine.* Berkeley: University of California Press, 1997.

Deitcher, David. *Dear Friends: American Photographs of Men Together, 1840–1918.* New York: Harry N. Abrams Inc., 2001.

Erkkila, Betsy. *Whitman the Political Poet.* New York: Oxford University Press, 1989.

Grossman, Allen. "The Poetics of Union in Whitman and Lincoln: An Inquiry Towards the Relationship of Art and Policy." In *The Ameri-*

can Renaissance Reconsidered, edited by Walter Benn Michaels and Donald E. Pease, 183–208, Baltimore: Johns Hopkins University Press, 1985.

Kaplan, Justin. *Walt Whitman: A Life*. New York: Simon and Schuster, 1980.

Katz, Jonathan Ned. *Love Stories: Sex Between Men Before Homosexuality*. Chicago: University of Chicago Press, 2001.

Kinney, Katherine. "Making Capital: War, Labor, and Whitman in Washington, D.C." In *Breaking Bounds: Whitman and American Cultural Studies*, edited by Betsy Erkkila and Jay Grossman, 174–189, New York: Oxford University Press, 1996.

Loving, Jerome. *Walt Whitman: The Song of Himself*. Berkeley: University of California Press, 1999.

Maslan, Mark. *Whitman Possessed: Poetry, Sexuality, and Popular Authority*. Baltimore: Johns Hopkins University Press, 2001.

Moon, Michael. *Disseminating Whitman: Revision and Corporeality in Leaves of Grass*. Cambridge: Harvard University Press, 1991.

Morris, Roy Jr. *The Better Angel: Walt Whitman in the Civil War*. New York: Oxford University Press, 2000.

Nelson, Robert K., and Kenneth M. Price. "Debating Manliness: Thomas Wentworth Higginson, William Sloane Kennedy, and the Question of Whitman." *American Literature* 73:3 (2001), 497–524.

Reynolds, David S. *Walt Whitman's America: A Cultural Biography*. New York: Knopf, 1995.

Shivley, Charley. *Drum Beats: Walt Whitman's Civil War Boy Lovers*. San Francisco: Gay Sunshine Press, 1989.

Sweet, Timothy. *Traces of War: Poetry, Photography, and the Crisis of the Union*. Baltimore: Johns Hopkins University Press, 1990.

Thomas, M. Wynn. "Fratricide and Brotherly Love: Whitman and the Civil War." In *The Cambridge Companion to Walt Whitman*, edited by Ezra Greenspan, 27–44, New York: Cambridge University Press, 1995.

Whitman, Walt. *Walt Whitman: The Correspondence, Vol. 1: 1842–1867*, edited by Edwin Haviland Miller. New York: New York University Press, 1961.

Winthrop, John. "A Modell of Christian Charity." In *The Puritans*, edited by Perry Miller and Thomas H. Johnson, 197–199, New York: American Book Company, 1938.

Wilson, Edmund. *Patriotic Gore: Studies in the Literature of the American Civil War*. New York: Farrar, Straus, and Giroux, 1962.

See also online

"Poet at Work: Recovered Notebooks from the Thomas Biggs Harned Walt Whitman Collection," as part of the Library of Congress' "American Memory" project, at http://memory.loc.gov/ammem/wwhtml/wwhome.html.

Price, Kenneth M., Martin G. Murray, and Robert K. Nelson, "Whitman's Memory," at http://www.iath.virginia.edu/fdw/volume2/price.

MEMORANDA

During the War.

BY WALT WHITMAN.

———

Author's Publication.

CAMDEN, NEW JERSEY.

1875—'76.

ABOUT THIS EDITION

This book reproduces the first edition of Memoranda During the War *found, in multiple copies, in the Library of Congress's rare book collections. The alterations, unless otherwise noted in the annotations, are solely with regard to the placement and orthography of the headings.*

∞✤∞

Memoranda, &c.

Duuring the Union War I commenced at the close of 1862, and continued steadily through '63, '64 and '65, to visit the sick and wounded of the Army, both on the field and in the Hospitals in and around Washington city. From the first I kept little note-books for impromptu jottings in pencil to refresh my memory of names and circumstances, and what was specially wanted, &c. In these I brief'd cases, persons, sights, occurrences in camp, by the bedside, and not seldom by the corpses of the dead. Of the present Volume most of its pages are *verbatim* renderings from such pen-cillings on the spot. Some were scratch'd down from narratives I heard and itemized while watching, or waiting, or tending some-body amid those scenes. I have perhaps forty such little note-books left, forming a special history of those years, for myself alone, full of associations never to be possibly said or sung. I wish I could convey to the reader the associations that attach to these soil'd and creas'd little livraisons, each composed of a sheet or two of paper, folded small to carry in the pocket, and fasten'd with a pin. I leave them just as I threw them by during the War, blotch'd here and there with more than one blood-stain, hurriedly written, sometimes at the clinique, not seldom amid the excitement of uncertainty, or defeat, or of action, or getting ready for it, or a march. Even these days, at the lapse of many years, I can never turn their tiny leaves, or even take one in my hand, without the actual army sights and hot emotions of the time rushing like a river in full tide through me. Each line, each scrawl, each memorandum, has its history. Some pang of anguish—some tragedy, profounder than ever poet wrote. Out of them arise active and breathing forms. They summon up, even in this silent and vacant room as I write, not only the sinewy regiments and brigades, marching or in camp, but the countless phantoms of those who fell and were hastily buried by wholesale in the battle-pits, or whose dust and bones have been since removed to the National Cemeteries of the land, especially through Virginia and Tennessee. (Not Northern soldiers only—many indeed the Carolinian, Georgian, Alabamian, Louisianian, Virginian—many a Southern face and form, pale, emaciated, with that strange tie of confidence and love between us, welded by sickness, pain of wounds, and little daily, nightly offices of nursing and friendly words and visits, comes up amid the rest, and does not mar, but rounds and gives a finish to the meditation.) Vivid as life, they recall and identify the long Hospital Wards, with their myriad-varied scenes of day or night—the graphic incidents of field or camp—the night before the battle, with many solemn yet cool preparations—the changeful exaltations and depressions of those four years, North and South—the convulsive memories, (let but a word, a broken sentence, serve to recall them) — the clues already quite vanish'd, like some old dream, and yet the list significant enough to soldiers — the scrawl'd, worn slips of paper that came up by bushels from the Southern prisons, Salisbury or Andersonville, by the hands of exchanged prisoners — the clank of crutches on the pavements or floors of Washington, or up and down the stairs of the Paymasters' offices — the Grand Review of homebound veterans at the close of the War, cheerily marching day after day by the President's house, one brigade succeeding another until it seem'd as if they would never end — the strange squads of Southern deserters, (*escapees,* I call'd them ;) — that little *genre* group, unreck'd amid the mighty whirl, I remember passing in a hospital corner, of a dying Irish boy, a Catholic priest, and an improvised altar — Four years compressing centuries of native passion, first-class pictures, tempests of life and death — an inexhaustible mine for the Histories, Drama, Romance and even Philosophy of centuries to come — indeed the Verteber of Poetry and Art, (of personal character too,) for all future America, (far more grand, in my opinion, to the hands capable of it, than Homer's siege of Troy, or the French wars to Shakspere ;) — and looking over all, in my remembrance, the tall form of President Lincoln, with his face of deep-cut lines, with the large, kind, canny eyes, the complexion of dark brown, and the tinge of wierd melancholy saturating all.

More and more, in my recollections of that period, and through its varied, multitudinous oceans and murky whirls, appear the central resolution and sternness of the bulk of the average American People, animated in Soul by a definite purpose, though sweeping and fluid as some great storm — the

Common People, emblemised in thousands of specimens of first-class Heroism, steadily accumulating, (no regiment, no company, hardly a file of men, North or South, the last three years, without such first-class specimens).

I know not how it may have been, or may be, to others—to me the main interest of the War, I found, (and still, on recollection, find,) in those specimens, and in the ambulance, the Hospital, and even the dead on the field. To me, the points illustrating the latent Personal Character and eligibilities of These States, in the two or three millions of American young and middle-aged men, North and South, embodied in the armies—and especially the one-third or one-fourth of their number, stricken by wounds or disease at some time in the course of the contest—were of more significance even than the Political interests involved. (As so much of a Race depends on what it thinks of death, and how it stands personal anguish and sickness. As, in the glints of emotions under emergencies, and the indirect traits and asides in Plutarch, &c., we get far profounder clues to the antique world than all its more formal history.)

Future years will never know the seething hell and the black infernal background of countless minor scenes and interiors, (not the few great battles) of the Secession War ; and it is best they should not. In the mushy influences of current times the fervid atmosphere and typical events of those years are in danger of being totally forgotten.[1] I have at night watch'd by the side of a sick man in the hospital, one who could not live many hours. I have seen his eyes flash and burn as he recurr'd to the cruelties on his surrender'd brother, and mutilations of the corpse afterward. [See, in the following pages, the incident at Upperville—

the seventeen, kill'd as in the description, were left there on the ground. After they dropt dead, no one touch'd them—all were made sure of, however. The carcasses were left for the citizens to bury or not, as they chose.]

Such was the War. It was not a quadrille in a ball-room. Its interior history will not only never be written, its practicality, minutia of deeds and passions, will never be even suggested. The actual Soldier of 1862–'65, North and South, with all his ways, his incredible dauntlessness, habits, practices, tastes, language, his appetite, rankness, his superb strength and animality, lawless gait, and a hundred unnamed lights and shades of camp—I say, will never be written—perhaps must not and should not be.

The present Memoranda may furnish a few stray glimpses into that life, and into those lurid interiors of the period, never to be fully convey'd to the future. For that purpose, and for what goes along with it, the Hospital part of the drama from '61 to '65, deserves indeed to be recorded—(I but suggest it.) Of that many-threaded drama, with its sudden and strange surprises, its confounding of prophecies, its moments of despair, the dread of foreign interference, the interminable campaigns, the bloody battles, the mighty and cumbrous and green armies, the drafts and bounties—the immense money expenditure, like a heavy pouring constant rain—with, over the whole land, the last three years of the struggle, an unending, universal mourning-wail of women, parents, orphans—the marrow of the tragedy concentrated in those Hospitals—(it seem'd sometimes as if the whole interest of the land, North and South, was one vast central Hospital, and all the rest of the affair but flanges)—those forming the Untold and Unwritten History of the War—infinitely greater (like Life's) than the few scraps and distortions that are ever told or written. Think how much, and of importance, will be—how much, civic and military, has already been—buried in the grave, in eternal darkness !.......But to my Memoranda.

FALMOUTH, VA.,
opposite Fredericksburgh, December 21, 1862.

Began my visits among the Camp Hospitals in the Army of the Potomac. Spent a good part of the day in a large brick mansion, on the banks of the Rappahannock, used as a Hospital since the battle—Seems to have receiv'd only the worst cases.[2] Out doors, at the foot of a tree, within ten yards of the front of the house, I notice a heap of amputated feet, legs, arms, hands, &c., a full load for a one-horse cart. Several dead bodies lie near, each cover'd with its brown woollen blanket. In the door-yard, towards the river, are fresh graves, mostly of officers, their names on pieces of barrel-staves or broken board, stuck in the dirt. (Most of these bodies were subsequently taken up and transported North to their friends.)..........The large mansion is quite crowded, upstairs and down, everything impromptu, no system, all bad enough, but I have no doubt the best that can be done ; all the wounds pretty bad, some frightful, the men in their old clothes, unclean and bloody. Some of the wounded are rebel soldiers and officers, prisoners. One, a Mississippian—a captain— hit badly in leg, I talk'd with some time ; he ask'd me for papers, which I gave him. (I saw him three months afterward in Washington, with his leg amputated, doing well.)..........I went through the rooms, downstairs and up. Some of the men were dying. I had nothing to give at that visit, but wrote a few letters to folks home, mothers, &c. Also talk'd to three or four, who seem'd most susceptible to it, and needing it.

(Everything is quiet now, here about Falmouth and the Rappa-hannock, but there was noise enough a week or so ago. Probably the earth never shook by artificial means, nor the air reverberated, more than on that winter daybreak of eight or nine days since, when Gen. Burnside order'd all the batteries of the army to com-bine for the bombardment of Fredericksburgh. It was in its way the most magnificent and terrible spectacle, with all the adjunct of sound, throughout the War. The perfect hush of the just-ending night was suddenly broken by the first gun, and in an instant all the thunderers, big and little, were in full chorus, which they kept up without intermission for several hours.)

December 23 to 31.

The results of the late battles are exhibited everywhere about here in thousands of cases, (hundreds die every day,) in the Camp, Brigade, and Division Hospitals. These are merely tents, and sometimes very poor ones, the wounded lying on the ground, lucky if their blankets are spread on layers of pine or hemlock twigs or small leaves. No cots ; seldom even a mattress. It is pretty cold. The ground is frozen hard, and there is occa-sional snow. I go around from one case to another. I do not see that I do much good, but I cannot leave them. Once in a while some youngster holds on to me convulsively, and I do what I can for him ; at any rate, stop with him and sit near him for hours, if he wishes it.

Besides the hospitals, I also go occasionally on long tours through the camps, talking with the men, &c. Sometimes at night among the groups around the fires, in their shebang enclosures of bushes. These are curious shows, full of characters and groups. I soon get acquainted anywhere in camp, with officers or men, and am always well used. Sometimes I go down on picket with the regiments I know best.......As to rations, the army here at present seems to be tolerably well supplied, and the men have enough, such as it is, mainly salt pork and hard tack. Most of the regiments lodge in the flimsy little shelter-tents. A few have built themselves huts of logs and mud, with fireplaces.

WASHINGTON,
January, '63.

Left camp at Falmouth, with some wounded, a few days since, and came here by Aquia Creek railroad, and so on Government steamer up the Potomac.[3] Many wounded were with us on the cars and boat. The cars were just common platform ones. The railroad journey of ten or twelve miles was made mostly before sunrise. The soldiers guarding the road came out from their tents or shebangs of bushes with rumpled hair and half-awake look. Those on duty were walking their posts, some on banks over us, others down far below the level of the track. I saw large cavalry camps off the road. At Aquia Creek landing were numbers of wounded going North. While I waited some three hours, I went around among them. Several wanted word sent home to parents, brothers, wives, &c., which I did for them, (by mail the next day from Washington.) On the boat I had my hands full. One poor fellow died going up.

I am now remaining in and around Washington, daily visiting the hospitals.[4] Am much in Patent Office, Eighth street, H street, Armory Square and others. Am now able to do a little good, having money, (as almoner of others home,) and getting experience........To-day, Sunday afternoon and till nine in the evening, visited Campbell Hospital ; attended specially to one case in Ward 1 ; very sick with pleurisy and typhoid fever ; young man, farmer's son, D. F. Russell, Company E, Sixtieth New York ; downhearted and feeble ; a long time before he would take any interest ; wrote a letter home to his mother, in Malone, Franklin County, N.Y., at his request ; gave him some fruit and one or two other gifts ; envelop'd and directed his letter, &c. Then went thoroughly through Ward 6 ; observ'd every case in the Ward, without, I think, missing one ; gave perhaps from twenty to thirty persons, each one some little gift, such as oranges, apples, sweet crackers, figs, &c.

Thursday, Jan. 21.

Devoted the main part of the day to Armory Square Hospital ; went pretty thoroughly through Wards F, G, H, and I ; some

fifty cases in each Ward. In Ward F supplied the men throughout with writing paper and stamp'd envelope each ; distributed
in small portions, to proper subjects, a large jar of first-rate pre-
serv'd berries, which had been donated to me by a lady—her
own cooking. Found several cases I thought good subjects for
small sums of money, which I furnish'd. (The wounded men
often come up broke, and it helps their spirits to have even the
small sum I give them.) My paper and envelopes all gone, but
distributed a good lot of amusing reading matter ; also, as I
thought judicious, tobacco, oranges, apples, &c. Interesting
cases in Ward I ; Charles Miller, bed No. 19, Company D,
Fifty-third Pennsylvania, is only sixteen years of age, very
bright, courageous boy, left leg amputated below the knee ;
next bed to him, another young lad very sick ; gave each appropriate gifts. In the bed above, also, amputation of the left leg ;
gave him a little jar of raspberries ; bed No. 1, this Ward, gave a
small sum ; also to a soldier on crutches, sitting on his bed
near.......(I am more and more surprised at the very great proportion of youngsters from fifteen to twenty-one in the army. I
afterwards found a still greater proportion among the Southerners.)

Evening, same day, went to see D. F. R., before alluded to ;
found him remarkably changed for the better ; up and
dress'd—quite a triumph ; he afterwards got well, and went
back to his regiment.........Distributed in the Wards a quantity of note-paper, and forty or fifty stamp'd envelopes, of
which I had recruited my stock, and the men were much in
need.

Fifty Hours Left Wounded on the Field.

Here is a case of a soldier I found among the crowded cots in the Patent Office. He likes to have some one to talk to, and we will listen to him. He got badly hit in his leg and side at Fredericksburgh that eventful Saturday, 13th of December. He lay the succeeding two days and nights helpless on the field, between the city and those grim terraces of batteries ; his company and regiment had been compell'd to leave him to his fate. To make matters worse, it happen'd he lay with his head slightly down hill, and could not help himself. At the end of some fifty hours he was brought off, with other wounded, under a flag of truce..........I ask him how the rebels treated him as he lay during those two days and nights within reach of them—whether they came to him—whether they abused him ? He answers that several of the rebels, soldiers and others, came to him, at one time and another. A couple of them, who were together, spoke roughly and sarcastically, but nothing worse. One middle-aged man, however, who seem'd to be moving around the field, among the dead and wounded, for benevolent purposes, came to him in a way he will never forget ; treated our soldier kindly, bound up his wounds, cheer'd him, gave him a couple of biscuits, and a drink of whiskey and water ; ask'd him if he could eat some beef. This good Secesh, however, did not change our soldier's position, for it might have caused the blood to burst from the wounds, clotted and stagnated. Our soldier is from Pennsylvania ; has had a pretty severe time ; the wounds proved to be bad ones. But he retains a good heart, and is at present on the gain.........(It is not uncommon for the men to remain on the field this way, one, two, or even four or five days.)

Letter Writing.

When eligible, I encourage the men to write, and myself, when call'd upon, write all sorts of letters for them, (including love let- ters, very tender ones.) Almost as I reel off this memoranda, I write for a new patient to his wife. M. de F., of the Seventeenth Connecticut, Company H, has just come up (February 17) from Windmill Point, and is received Ward H, Armory Square. He is an intelligent looking man, has a foreign accent, black-eyed and hair'd, a Hebraic appearance. Wants a telegraphic message sent to his wife, New Canaan, Ct. I agree to send the message—but to make things sure, I also sit down and write the wife a letter, and despatch it to the post-office immediately, as he fears she will come on, and he does not wish her to, as he will surely get well.

Saturday, Jan. 30.

Afternoon, visited Campbell Hospital. Scene of cleaning up the Ward, and giving the men all clean clothes—through the Ward (6) the patients dressing or being dress'd—the naked upper half of the bodies—the good-humor and fun—the shirts, drawers, sheets of beds, &c., and the general fixing up for Sunday. Gave J. L. 50 cts.

Wednesday, Feb. 4th.

Visited Armory Square Hospital, went pretty thoroughly through Wards E and D. Supplied paper and envelopes to all who wish'd—as usual, found plenty of the men who needed those articles. Wrote letters. Saw and talk'd with two or three members of the Brooklyn Fourteenth.........A poor fellow in Ward D, with a fearful wound in a fearful condition, was having some loose splinters of bone taken from the neighborhood of the wound. The operation was long, and one of great pain—yet, after it was well commenced, the soldier bore it in silence. He sat up, propp'd—was much wasted—had lain a long time quiet in one position, (not for days only, but weeks,)—a bloodless, brown-skinn'd face, with eyes full of determination—belong'd to a New York regiment. There was an unusual cluster of surgeons, medical cadets, nurses, &c., around his bed—I thought the whole thing was done with tenderness, and done well.

In one case, the wife sat by the side of her husband, his sickness, typhoid fever, pretty bad. In another, by the side of her son—a mother—she told me she had seven children, and this was the youngest. (A fine, kind, healthy, gentle mother, good-looking, not very old, with a cap on her head, and dress'd like home—what a charm it gave to the whole Ward.) I liked the woman "nurse in Ward E"—I noticed how she sat a long time by a poor fellow who just had, that morning, in addition to his other sickness, bad hemmorhage—she gently assisted him, reliev'd him of the blood, holding a cloth to his mouth, as he cough'd it up—he was so weak he could only just turn his head over on the pillow.

One young New York man, with a bright, handsome face, had been lying several months from a most disagreeable wound, receiv'd at Bull Run. A bullet had shot him right through the bladder, hitting him front, low in the belly, and coming out back. He had suffer'd much—the water came out of the wound, by slow but steady quantities, for many weeks—so that he lay almost constantly in a sort of puddle—and there were other disagreeable circumstances. He was of good heart, however. At present comparatively comfortable ; had a bad throat, was delighted with a stick of horehound candy I gave him, with one or two other trifles.

Feb. 23.

I must not let the great Hospital at the Patent Office pass away without some mention. A few weeks ago the vast area of the second story of that noblest of Washington buildings, was crowded close with rows of sick, badly wounded and dying soldiers. They were placed in three very large apartments. I went there many times. It was a strange, solemn and, with all its features of suffering and death, a sort of fascinating sight. I go sometimes at night to soothe and relieve particular cases. Two of the immense apartments are fill'd with high and ponderous glass cases, crowded with models in miniature of every kind of utensil, machine or invention, it ever enter'd into the mind of man to conceive ; and with curiosities and foreign presents. Between these cases are lateral openings, perhaps eight feet wide, and quite deep, and in these were placed the sick ; besides a great long double row of them up and down through the middle of the hall. Many of them were very bad cases, wounds and amputations. Then there was a gallery running above the hall, in which there were beds also. It was, indeed, a curious scene at night, when lit up. The glass cases, the beds, the forms lying there, the gallery above, and the marble pavement under foot— the suffering, and the fortitude to bear it in various degrees— occasionally, from some, the groan that could not be repress'd—sometimes a poor fellow dying, with emaciated face and glassy eye, the nurse by his side, the doctor also there, but no friend, no relative—such were the sights but lately in the Patent Office. The wounded have since been removed from there, and it is now vacant again.

The White House,
by Moonlight—Feb. 24.

A spell of fine soft weather. I wander about a good deal, especially at night, under the moon. To-night took a long look at the President's House—and here is my splurge about it. The white portico—the brilliant gas-light shining—the palace-like portico—the tall, round columns, spotless as snow—the walls also—the tender and soft moonlight, flooding the pale marble, and making peculiar faint languishing shades, not shadows—everywhere too a soft transparent haze, a thin blue moon-lace, hanging in the night in the air—the brilliant and extra plentiful clusters of gas, on and around the facade, columns, portico, &c.—everything so white, so marbly pure and dazzling, yet soft—the White House of future poems, and of dreams and dramas, there in the soft and copious moon—the pure and gorgeous front, in the trees, under the night-lights, under the lustrous flooding moon, full of reality, full of illusion—The forms of the trees, leafless, silent, in trunk and myriad-angles of branches, under the stars and sky—the White House of the land, the White House of the night, and of beauty and silence—sentries at the gates, and by the portico, silent, pacing there in blue overcoats—stopping you not at all, but eyeing you with sharp eyes, whichever way you move.

An Army Hospital Ward.

Let me specialize a visit I made to the collection of barrack-like one-story edifices, call'd Campbell Hospital, out on the flats, at the end of the then horse-railway route, on Seventh street. There is a long building appropriated to each Ward. Let us go into Ward 6. It contains to-day, I should judge, eighty or a hundred patients, half sick, half wounded. The edifice is nothing but boards, well whitewash'd inside, and the usual slender-framed iron bedsteads, narrow and plain. You walk down the central passage, with a row on either side, their feet toward you, and their heads to the wall. There are fires in large stoves, and the prevailing white of the walls is reliev'd by some ornaments, stars, circles, &c., made of evergreens. The view of the whole edifice and occupants can be taken at once, for there is no partition. You may hear groans, or other sounds of unendurable suffering, from two or three of the iron cots, but in the main there is quiet—almost a painful absence of demonstration ; but the pallid face, the dull'd eye, and the moisture on the lip, are demonstration enough. Most of these sick or hurt are evidently young fellows from the country, farmers' sons, and such like. Look at the fine large frames, the bright and broad countenances, and the many yet lingering proofs of strong constitution and physique. Look at the patient and mute manner of our American wounded, as they lie in such a sad collection ; representatives from all New England, and from New York and New Jersey and Pennsylvania—indeed, from all the States and all the cities— largely from the West. Most of them are entirely without friends or acquaintances here—no familiar face, and hardly a word of judicious sympathy or cheer, through their sometimes long and tedious sickness, or the pangs of aggravated wounds.

A Connecticut Case.

This young man in bed 25 is H. D. B., of the Twenty-seventh Connecticut, Company B. His folks live at Northford, near New Haven. Though not more than twenty-one, or thereabouts, he has knock'd much around the world, on sea and land, and has seen some fighting on both. When I first saw him he was very sick, with no appetite. He declined offers of money—said he did not need anything. As I was quite anxious to do something, he confess'd that he had a hankering for a good home-made rice pudding—thought he could relish it better than anything. At this time his stomach was very weak. (The doctor, whom I consulted, said nourishment would do him more good than anything ; but things in the hospital, though better than usual, revolted him.) I soon procured B. his rice-pudding. A Washington lady, (Mrs. O'C.), hearing his wish, made the pudding herself, and I took it up to him the next day. He subsequently told me he lived upon it for three or four days.......This B. is a good sample of the American Eastern young man—the typical Yankee. I took a fancy to him, and gave him a nice pipe, for a keepsake. He receiv'd afterwards a box of things from home, and nothing would do but I must take dinner with him, which I did, and a very good one it was.

Two Brooklyn Boys.

Here in this same Ward are two young men from Brooklyn, members of the Fifty-first New York.[5] I had known both the two as young lads at home, so they seem near to me. One of them, J. L., lies there with an amputated arm, the stump healing pretty well. (I saw him lying on the ground at Fredericksburgh last December, all bloody, just after the arm was taken off. He was very phlegmatic about it, munching away at a cracker in the remaining hand—made no fuss.) He will recover, and thinks and talks yet of meeting the Johnny Rebs.

A Secesh Brave.

The brave, grand soldiers are not comprised in those of one side, any more than the other. Here is a sample of an unknown Southerner, a lad of seventeen. At the War Department, a few days ago, I witness'd a presentation of captured flags to the Secretary. Among others a soldier named Gant, of the One Hundred and Fourth Ohio Volunteers, presented a rebel battle-flag, which one of the officers stated to me was borne to the mouth of our cannon and planted there by a boy but seventeen years of age, who actually endeavor'd to stop the muzzle of the gun with fence-rails. He was kill'd in the effort, and the flag-staff was sever'd by a shot from one of our men. (Perhaps, in that Southern boy of seventeen, untold in history, unsung in poems, altogether unnamed, fell as strong a spirit, and as sweet, as any in all time.)

The Wounded from Chancellorsville, May, '63.

As I write this, the wounded have begun to arrive from Hooker's command from bloody Chancellorsville.[6] I was down among the first arrivals. The men in charge of them told me the bad cases were yet to come. If that is so I pity them, for these are bad enough. You ought to see the scene of the wounded arriving at the landing here foot of Sixth street, at night. Two boat loads came about half-past seven last night. A little after eight it rain'd a long and violent shower. The poor, pale, helpless soldiers had been debark'd, and lay around on the wharf and neighborhood anywhere. The rain was, probably, grateful to them ; at any rate they were exposed to it. The few torches light up the spectacle. All around—on the wharf, on the ground, out on side places— the men are lying on blankets, old quilts, &c., with bloody rags bound round heads, arms, and legs. The attendants are few, and at night few outsiders also—only a few hard-work'd transporta- tion men and drivers. (The wounded are getting to be common, and people grow callous.) The men, whatever their condition, lie there, and patiently wait till their turn comes to be taken up. Near by, the ambulances are now arriving in clusters, and one after another is call'd to back up and take its load. Extreme cases are sent off on stretchers. The men generally make little or no ado, whatever their sufferings. A few groans that cannot be sup- press'd, and occasionally a scream of pain as they lift a man into the ambulance........To day, as I write, hundreds more are expected, and to-morrow and the next day more, and so on for many days. Quite often they arrive at the rate of 1000 a day.

May 12—A Night Battle, over a week since.

We already talk of Histories of the War, (presently to accumu- late)—yes—technical histories of some things, statistics, official reports, and so on—but shall we ever get histories of the *real* things ?.......There was part of the late battle at Chancellorsville,

(second Fredericksburgh,) a little over a week ago, Saturday,
Saturday night and Sunday, under Gen. Joe Hooker, I would
like to give just a glimpse of—(a moment's look in a terrible
storm at sea—of which a few suggestions are enough, and full
details impossible.) The fighting had been very hot during the
day, and after an intermission the latter part, was resumed at
night, and kept up with furious energy till 3 o'clock in the morning. That afternoon (Saturday) an attack sudden and strong by
Stonewall Jackson had gain'd a great advantage to the Southern
army, and broken our lines, entering us like a wedge, and leaving
things in that position at dark. But Hooker at 11 at night made a
desperate push, drove the Secesh forces back, restored his original lines, and resumed his plans. This night scrimmage was very
exciting, and afforded countless strange and fearful pictures. The
fighting had been general both at Chancellorsville and northeast
at Fredericksburgh. (We hear of some poor fighting, episodes,
skedaddling on our part. I think not of it. I think of the fierce
bravery, the general rule.) One Corps, the 6th, Sedgewick's,
fights four dashing and bloody battles in 36 hours, retreating in
great jeopardy, losing largely and maintaining itself, fighting
with the sternest desperation under all circumstances, getting
over the Rappahannock only by the skin of its teeth, yet getting
over. It lost many, many brave men, yet it took vengeance,
ample vengeance.

But it was the tug of Saturday evening, and through the
night and Sunday morning, I wanted to make a special note of.
It was largely in the woods, and quite a general engagement.
The night was very pleasant, at times the moon shining out full
and clear, all Nature so calm in itself, the early summer grass so

rich, and foliage of the trees—yet there the battle raging, and many good fellows lying helpless, with new accessions to them, and every minute amid the rattle of muskets and crash of cannon, (for there was an artillery contest too,) the red life-blood oozing out from heads or trunks or limbs upon that green and dew-cool grass. The woods take fire, and many of the wounded, unable to move, (especially some of the divisions in the Sixth Corps,) are consumed—quite large spaces are swept over, burning the dead also—some of the men have their hair and beards singed—some, splatches of burns on their faces and hands—others holes burnt in their clothing........The flashes of fire from the cannon, the quick flaring flames and smoke, and the immense roar—the musketry so general, the light nearly bright enough for each side to see one another—the crashing, tramping of men—the yelling—close quarters—we hear the Secesh yells—our men cheer loudly back, especially if Hooker is in sight—hand to hand conflicts, each side stands to it, brave, determin'd as demons, they often charge upon us—a thousand deeds are done worth to write newer greater poems on—and still the woods on fire—still many are not only scorch'd—too many, unable to move, are burn'd to death........Then the camp of the wounded—O heavens, what scene is this ?—is this indeed *humanity*—these butchers' shambles ? There are several of them. There they lie, in the largest, in an open space in the woods, from 500 to 600 poor fellows—the groans and screams—the odor of blood, mixed with the fresh scent of the night, the grass, the trees—that Slaughter-house !—O well is it their mothers, their sisters cannot see them—cannot conceive, and never conceiv'd, these things........One man is shot by a shell, both in the arm and leg—both are amputated—there lie the rejected members. Some have their legs blown off—some bullets through the breast—some indescribably horrid wounds in the face or head, all mutilated, sickening, torn, gouged out— some in the abdomen—some mere boys—here is one his face colorless as chalk, lying perfectly still, a bullet has perforated the abdomen—life is ebbing fast, there is no help for him. In the camp of the wounded are many rebels, badly hurt—they take their regular turns with the rest, just the same as any—the sur- geons use them just the same.........Such is the camp of the wounded—such a fragment, a reflection afar off of the bloody scene—while over all the clear, large moon comes out at times softly, quietly shining.

Such, amid the woods, that scene of flitting souls—amid the crack and crash and yelling sounds—the impalpable perfume of the woods—and yet the pungent, stifling smoke—shed with the radiance of the moon, the round, maternal queen, looking from heaven at intervals so placid—the sky so heavenly—the clear- obscure up there, those buoyant upper oceans—a few large placid stars beyond, coming out and then disappearing—the melancholy, draperied night above, around.......And there, upon the roads, the fields, and in those woods, that contest, never one more desperate in any age or land—both parties now in force— masses—no fancy battle, no semi-play, but fierce and savage demons fighting there—courage and scorn of death the rule, exceptions almost none.

What history, again I say, can ever give—for who can know, the mad, determin'd tussle of the armies, in all their separate large and little squads—as this—each steep'd from crown to toe in desperate, mortal purports ? Who know the conflict hand-to-hand—the many conflicts in the dark, those shadowy-tangled, flashing-moonbeam'd woods—the writhing groups and squads—hear through the woods the cries, the din, the cracking guns and pistols—the distant cannon—the cheers and calls, and threats and awful music of the oaths—the indiscribable mix—the officers' orders, persuasions, encouragements—the devils fully rous'd in human hearts—the strong word, *Charge, men, charge*—the flash of the naked sword, and many a flame and smoke—And still the broken, clear and clouded heaven—and still again the moonlight pouring silvery soft its radiant patches over all ?.........Who paint the scene, the sudden partial panic of the afternoon, at dusk ? Who paint the irrepressible advance of the Second Division of the Third Corps, under Hooker himself, suddenly order'd up—those rapid-filing phantoms through the woods ? Who show what moves there in the shadows, fluid and firm—to save, (and it did save,) the Army's name, perhaps the Nation ? And there the veterans hold the field. (Brave Berry falls not yet—but Death has mark'd him—soon he falls.)

Of scenes like these, I say, who writes—who e'er can write, the story ? Of many a score—aye, thousands, North and South, of unwrit heroes, unknown heroisms, incredible, impromptu, first-class desperations—who tells ? No history, ever—No poem sings, nor music sounds, those bravest men of all—those deeds. No formal General's report, nor print, nor book in the library, nor column in the paper, embalms the bravest, North or South, East or West. Unnamed, unknown, remain, and still remain, the bravest soldiers. Our manliest—our boys—our hardy darlings. Indeed no picture gives them. Likely their very names are lost.

Likely, the typic one of them, (standing, no doubt, for hundreds, thousands,) crawls aside to some bush-clump, or ferny tuft, on receiving his death-shot—there, sheltering a little while, soaking roots, grass and soil with red blood—the battle advances, retreats, flits from the scene, sweeps by—and there, haply with pain and suffering, (yet less, far less, than is supposed,) the last lethargy winds like a serpent round him—the eyes glaze in death—none recks—Perhaps the burial-squads, in truce, a week afterwards, search not the secluded spot—And there, at last, the Bravest Soldier crumbles in the soil of mother earth, unburied and unknown.

June 18.

In one of the Hospitals I find Thomas Haley, Co. M, Fourth New York Cavalry—a regular Irish boy, a fine specimen of youthful physical manliness—shot through the lungs—inevitably dying—came over to this country from Ireland to enlist—has not a single friend or acquaintance here—is sleeping soundly at this moment, (but it is the sleep of death)—has a bullet-hole straight through the lung.......I saw Tom when first brought here, three days since, and didn't suppose he could live twelve hours—(yet he looks well enough in the face to a casual observer.) He lies there with his frame exposed above the waist, all naked, for coolness, a fine built man, the tan not yet bleach'd from his cheeks and neck. It is useless to talk to him, as with his sad hurt, and the stimulants they give him, and the utter strangeness of every object, face, furniture, &c., the poor fellow, even when awake, is like a frighten'd, shy animal. Much of the time he sleeps, or half sleeps. (Sometimes I thought he knew more than he show'd.) I often come and sit by him in perfect silence ; he will breathe for ten minutes as softly and evenly as a young babe asleep. Poor youth, so handsome, athletic, with profuse beautiful shining hair. One time as I sat looking at him while he lay asleep, he suddenly, without the least start, awaken'd, open'd his eyes, gave me a long, long steady look, turning his face very slightly to gaze easier—one long, clear silent look—a slight sigh—then turn'd back and went into his doze again. Little he knew, poor death-stricken boy, the heart of the stranger that hover'd near.

W. H. E., Co. F., Second N. J.

His disease is pneumonia. He lay sick at the wretched hospital below Aquia Creek, for seven or eight days before brought here. He was detail'd from his regiment to go there and help as nurse ; but was soon taken down himself. Is an elderly, sallow-faced, rather gaunt, gray-hair'd man ; a widower, with children. He express'd a great desire for good, strong, green tea. An excellent lady, Mrs. W., of Washington, soon sent him a package ; also a small sum of money. The doctor said give him the tea at pleasure ; it lay on the table by his side, and he used it every day. He slept a great deal ; could not talk much, as he grew deaf. Occupied bed 15, Ward I, Armory. (The same lady above, Mrs. W., sent the men a large package of tobacco.)

J. G. lies in bed 52, Ward I ; is of Co. B, Seventh Pennsylvania.

I gave him a small sum of money, some tobacco and envelopes. To a man adjoining, also gave 25 cents ; he flush'd in the face, when I offer'd it—refused at first, but as I found he had not a cent, and was very fond of having the daily papers, to read, I prest it on him. He was evidently very grateful, but said little.

J. T. L., of Co. F., Ninth New Hampshire, lies in bed 37, Ward I. Is very fond of tobacco. I furnish him some ; also with a little money. Has gangrene of the feet, a pretty bad case ; will surely have to lose three toes. Is a regular specimen of an old-fashion'd, rude, hearty, New England country man, impressing me with his likeness to that celebrated singed cat, who was better than she look'd.

Bed 3, Ward E, Armory, has a great hankering for pickles, something pungent. After consulting the doctor, I gave him a small bottle of horse-radish ; also some apples ; also a book.........Some of the nurses are excellent. The woman nurse in this Ward I like very much. (Mrs. Wright—a year afterwards I found her in Mansion House Hospital, Alexandri—she is a perfect nurse.)

In one bed a young man, Marcus Small, Co. K, Seventh Maine—sick with dysentery and typhoid fever—pretty critical, too—I talk with him often—he thinks he will die—looks like it indeed. I write a letter for him home to East Livermore, Maine—I let him talk to me a little, but not much, advise him to keep very quiet—do most of the talking myself—stay quite a while with him, as he holds to my hand—talk to him in a cheering, but slow, low, and measured manner—talk about his furlough, and going home as soon as he is able to travel.

Thomas Lindly, First Pennsylvania Cavalry, shot very badly through the foot—poor young man, he suffers horribly, has to be constantly dosed with morphine, his face ashy and glazed, bright young eyes—give him a large handsome apple, tell him to have it roasted in the morning, as he generally feels easier then, and can eat a little breakfast. I write two letters for him.

Opposite, an old Quaker lady is sitting by the side of her son, Amer Moore, Second U.S. Artillery—shot in the head two weeks since, very low, quite rational—from hips down, paralyzed—he will surely die. I speak a very few words to him every day and evening—he answers pleasantly—is a handsome fellow—wants nothing—(he told me soon after he came about his home affairs, his mother had been an invalid, and he fear'd to let her know his condition.) He died soon after she came.

(In my visits to the Hospitals I found it was in the simple matter of Personal Presence, and emanating ordinary cheer and magnetism, that I succeeded and help'd more than by medical nursing, or delicacies, or gifts of money, or anything else. During the war I possess'd the perfection of physical health. My habit, when practicable, was to prepare for starting out on one of those daily or nightly tours, of from a couple to four or five hours, by fortifying myself with previous rest, the bath, clean clothes, a good meal, and as cheerful an appearance as possible.)

June 25, (Thursday, Sundown).

As I sit writing this paragraph I see a train of about thirty huge four-horse wagons, used as ambulances, fill'd with wounded, passing up Fourteenth street, on their way, probably, to Columbian, Carver, and Mount Pleasant Hospitals. This is the way the men come in now, seldom in small numbers, but almost always in these long, sad processions. Through the past winter, while our army lay opposite Fredericksburgh, the like strings of ambulances were of frequent occurrence along Seventh street, passing slowly up from the steamboat wharf, with loads from Aquia Creek.

Bad Wounds, the Young.

The soldiers are nearly all young men, and far more American than is generally supposed—I should say nine-tenths are native-born. Among the arrivals from Chancellorsville I find a large proportion of Ohio, Indiana, and Illinois men. As usual, there are all sorts of wounds. Some of the men fearfully burnt from the explosion of artillery caissons. One Ward has a long row of officers, some with ugly hurts. Yesterday was perhaps worse than usual. Amputations are going on—the attendants are dressing wounds. As you pass by, you must be on your guard where you look. I saw the other day a gentleman, a visitor apparently from curiosity, in one of the Wards, stop and turn a moment to look at an awful wound they were probing, &c. He turn'd pale, and in a moment more he had fainted away and fallen on the floor.

June 29.

Just before sundown this evening a very large cavalry force went by—a fine sight. The men evidently had seen service. First came a mounted band of sixteen bugles, drums and cymbals, playing wild martial tunes—made my heart jump. Then the principal officers, then company after company, with their officers at their heads, making of course the main part of the cavalcade ; then a long train of men with led horses, lots of mounted negroes with special horses—and a long string of baggage-waggons, each drawn by four horses—and then a motley rear guard. It was a pronouncedly warlike and gay show. The sabres clank'd, the men look'd young and healthy and strong ; the electric tramping of so many horses on the hard road, and the gallant bearing, fine seat, and bright faced appearance of a thousand and more handsome young American men, were so good to see—quite set me up for hours.

An hour later another troop went by, smaller in numbers, perhaps three hundred men. They too look'd like serviceable men, campaigners used to field and fight.

July 3.

This forenoon, for more than an hour, again long strings of cavalry, several regiments, very fine men and horses, four or five abreast. I saw them in Fourteenth street, coming in town from north. Several hundred extra horses, some of the mares with colts, trotting along. (Appear'd to be a number of prisoners too.).........How inspiriting always the cavalry regiments ! Our men are generally well mounted, they ride well, feel good, are young, and gay on the saddle, their blankets in a roll behind them, their sabres clanking at their sides. This noise and movement and the tramp of many horses' hoofs has a curious effect upon one. The bugles play—presently you hear them afar off, deaden'd, mix'd with other noises.

Then just as they had all pass'd, a string of ambulances commenced from the other way, moving up Fourteenth street north, slowly wending along, bearing a large lot of wounded to the hospitals.

4th July—Battle of GETTYSBURG.

The weather to-day, upon the whole, is very fine, warm, but from a smart rain last night, fresh enough, and no dust, which is a great relief for this city. I saw the parade about noon, Pennsylvania avenue, from Fifteenth street down toward the Capitol. There were three regiments of infantry, (I suppose the ones doing patrol duty here,) two or three societies of Odd Fellows, a lot of children in barouches, and a squad of policemen. (It was a useless imposition upon the soldiers—they have work enough on their backs without piling the like of this.)

As I went down the Avenue, saw a big flaring placard on the bulletin board of a newspaper office, announcing "Glorious Victory for the Union Army !" Meade had fought Lee at Gettysburgh, Pennsylvania, yesterday and day before, and repuls'd him most signally, taken 3,000 prisoners, &c. (I afterwards saw Meade's despatch, very modest, and a sort of order of the day from the President himself, quite religious, giving thanks to the Supreme, and calling on people to do the same , &c.)[7]

I walk'd on to Armory Hospital—took along with me several bottles of blackberry and cherry syrup, good and strong, but innocent. Went through several of the Wards, announc'd to the soldiers the news from Meade, and gave them all a good drink of the syrups with ice water, quite refreshing.........Meanwhile the Washington bells are ringing their sundown peals for Fourth of July, and the usual fusillades of boys' pistols, crackers, and guns.

A Cavalry Camp.

I am writing this nearly sundown, watching a Cavalry company, (acting Signal Service,) just come in through a shower, and making their night's camp ready on some broad, vacant ground, a sort of hill, in full view, opposite my window. There are the men in their yellow-striped jackets. All are dismounted ; the freed horses stand with drooping heads and wet sides. They are to be led off presently in groups, to water. The little wall-tents and shelter-tents spring up quickly. I see the fires already blazing, and pots and kettles over them. The laggards among the men are driving in tent-poles, wielding their axes with strong, slow blows. I see great huddles of horses, bundles of hay, men, (some with unbuckled sabres yet on their sides,) a few officers, piles of wood, the flames of the fires, comrades by two and threes, saddles, harness, &c. The smoke streams upward, additional men arrive and dismount—some drive in stakes, and tie their horses to them ; some go with buckets for water, some are chopping wood, and so on.

July 6.

A steady rain, dark and thick and warm. A train of six-mule wagons has just pass'd bearing pontoons, great square-end flatboats, and the heavy planking for overlaying them. We hear that the Potomac above here is flooded, and are wondering whether Lee will be able to get back across again, or whether Meade will indeed break him to pieces.

The cavalry camp on the hill is a ceaseless field of observation for me. This forenoon there stand the horses, huddled, tether'd together, dripping, steaming, chewing their hay. The men emerge from their tents, dripping also. The fires are half quench'd.

July 10.

Still the camp opposite—perhaps 50 or 60 tents. Some of the men are cleaning their sabres, (pleasant to-day,) some brushing boots, some laying off, reading, writing—some cooking, some sleeping—On long temporary cross-sticks back of the tents are hung saddles and cavalry accoutrements—blankets and overcoats are hung out to air—there are the squads of horses tether'd, feeding, continually stamping and whisking their tails to keep off flies.......I sit long in my third story window and look at the scene—a hundred little things going on—or peculiar objects connected with the camp that could not be described, any one of them justly, without much minute drawing and coloring in words.

A New York Soldier.

This afternoon, July 22, I have spent a long time with Oscar F.
Wilber, Company G, One Hundred and Fifty-fourth New York,
low with chronic diarrhoea, and a bad wound also. He ask'd me
to read to him a chapter in the New Testament. I complied, and
ask'd him what I should read. He said : "Make your own
choice." I open'd at the close of one of the first books of the
Evangelists, and read the chapters describing the latter hours of
Christ, and the scenes at the crucifixion. The poor, wasted
young man ask'd me to read the following chapter also, how
Christ rose again. I read very slowly, for Oscar was feeble. It
pleas'd him very much, yet the tears were in his eyes. He ask'd
me if I enjoy'd religion. I said : "Perhaps not, my dear, in the
way you mean, and yet, may-be, it is the same thing." He said :
"It is my chief reliance." He talk'd of death, and said he did not
fear it. I said : "Why, Oscar, don't you think you will get well ?"
He said : "I may, but it is not probable." He spoke calmly of his
condition. The wound was very bad ; it discharg'd much. Then
the diarrhoea had prostrated him, and I felt that he was even
then the same as dying. He behaved very manly and affectionate. The kiss I gave him as I was about leaving he return'd four-
fold. He gave me his mother's address, Mrs. Sally D. Wilber,
Alleghany Post-office, Cattaraugus County, N. Y. I had several
such interviews with him. He died a few days after the one just
described.

Aug. 8.

To-night, as I was trying to keep cool, sitting by a wounded soldier in Armory Square, I was attracted by some pleasant singing
in an adjoining Ward. As my soldier was asleep, I left him, and
entering the Ward where the music was, I walk'd half way down
and took a seat by the cot of a young Brooklyn friend, S. R., badly
wounded in the hand at Chancellorsville, and who has suffer'd
much, but who at that moment in the evening was wide awake
and comparatively easy. He had turn'd over on his left side to get a
better view of the singers, but the plentiful drapery of the mus-
quito curtains of the adjoining cots obstructed the sight. I stept
round and loop'd them all up, so that he had a clear show, and
then sat down again by him, and look'd and listened. The principal singer was a young lady nurse of one of the Wards, accompanying on a melodeon, and join'd by the lady nurses of other
Wards. They sat there, making a charming group, with their
handsome, healthy faces ; and standing up a little behind them
were some ten or fifteen of the convalescent soldiers, young men,
nurses, &c., with books in their hands, taking part in the singing.
Of course it was not such a performance as the great soloists at the
New York Opera House take a hand in ; but I am not sure but I
receiv'd as much pleasure, under the circumstances, sitting there,
as I have had from the best Italian compositions, express'd by
world-famous performers.......The scene was, indeed, an impressive one. The men lying up and down the hospital, in their cots,

(some badly wounded—some never to rise thence,) the cots themselves, with their drapery of white curtains, and the shadows down the lower and upper parts of the Ward ; then the silence of the men, and the attitudes they took—the whole was a sight to look around upon again and again. And there, sweetly rose those female voices up to the high, whitewash'd wooden roof, and pleasantly the roof sent it all back again. They sang very well ; mostly quaint old songs and declamatory hymns, to fitting tunes. Here, for instance, is one of the songs they sang :

SHINING SHORES.

My days are swiftly gliding by, and I a Pilgrim stranger,
Would not detain them as they fly, those hours of toil and
    danger ;
For O we stand on Jordan's strand, our friends are passing
    over,
And just before, the shining shores we may almost discover.

We'll gird our loins my brethren dear, our distant home
    discerning,
Our absent Lord has left us word, let every lamp be burning,
For O we stand on Jordan's strand, our friends are passing
    over,
And just before, the shining shores we may almost discover.

As the strains reverberated through the great edifice of boards, (an excellent place for musical performers,) it was plain to see how it all sooth'd and was grateful to the men. I saw one

near me turn over, and bury his face partially in his pillow ; he
was probably ashamed to be seen with wet eyes.

Aug. 12.

I see the President almost every day, as I happen to live where he
passes to or from his lodgings out of town. He never sleeps at the
White House during the hot season, but has quarters at a healthy
location, some three miles north of the city, the Soldiers' Home, a
United States military establishment. I saw him this morning about
$8\frac{1}{2}$ coming in to business, riding on Vermont avenue, near L street.
The sight is a significant one, (and different enough from how and
where I first saw him.*) He always has a company of twenty-five or
thirty cavalry, with sabres drawn, and held upright over their shoulders. The party makes no great show in uniforms or horses. Mr. Lincoln, on the saddle, generally rides a good-sized easy-going gray

---

* I shall not easily forget the first time I saw Abraham Lincoln. It must
have been about the 18th or 19th of February, 1861. It was rather a pleasant spring afternoon, in New York city, as Lincoln arrived there from
the West to stop a few hours and then pass on to Washington, to prepare for his inauguration. I saw him in Broadway, near the site of the
present Post-office. He had come down, I think, from Canal street, to
stop at the Astor House. The broad spaces, sidewalks, and street in the
neighborhood, and for some distance, were crowded with solid masses
of people, many thousands. The omnibuses and other vehicles had been
all turn'd off, leaving an unusual hush in that busy part of the city.
Presently two or three shabby hack barouches made their way with
some difficulty through the crowd, and drew up at the Astor House
entrance. A tall figure step'd out of the centre of these barouches, paus'd
leisurely on the sidewalk, look'd up at the dark granite walls and loom-

horse, is dress'd in plain black, somewhat rusty and dusty ; wears a black stiff hat, and looks about as ordinary in attire, &c., as the commonest man. A Lieutenant, with yellow straps, rides at his left, and following behind, two by two, come the cavalry men in their yellow-striped jackets. They are generally going at a slow trot, as that is the pace set them by the One they wait upon. The sabres and accoutrements clank, and the entirely unornamental *cortege* as it trots towards Lafayette square, arouses no sensation, only some curious stranger stops and gazes. I see very plainly ABRAHAM LINCOLN'S dark brown face, with the deep cut lines, the eyes, &c., always to me

---

ing architecture of the grand old hotel—then, after a relieving stretch of the arms and legs, turn'd round for over a minute to slowly and good-humoredly scan the appearance of the vast and silent crowds—and so, with very moderate pace, and accompanied by a few unknown-looking persons, ascended the portico steps.

The figure, the look, the gait, are distinctly impress'd upon me yet ; the unusual and uncouth height, the dress of complete black, the stovepipe hat push'd back on the head, the dark-brown complexion, the seam'd and wrinkled yet canny-looking face, the black, bushy head of hair, the disproportionately long neck, and the hands held behind as he stood observing the people. All was comparative and ominous silence. The new comer look'd with curiosity upon that immense sea of faces, and the sea of faces return'd the look with similar curiosity. In both there was a dash of something almost comical. Yet there was much anxiety in certain quarters. Cautious persons had fear'd that there would be some outbreak, some mark'd indignity or insult to the President elect on his passage through the city, for he possess'd no personal popularity in New York, and not much political. No such outbreak or insult, however, occurr'd. Only the silence of the crowd was very significant to those who were accustom'd to the usual demonstrations of New York in wild, tumultuous hurrahs—the deafening tumults of welcome, and the thunder-shouts of pack'd myriads along the whole line of Broadway, receiving Hungarian Kossuth or Filibuster Walker.

with a deep latent sadness in the expression. We have got so that we always exchange bows, and very cordial ones.

Sometimes the President goes and comes in an open barouche. The cavalry always accompany him, with drawn sabres. Often I notice as he goes out evenings—and sometimes in the morning, when he returns early—he turns off and halts at the large and handsome residence of the Secretary of War, on K street, and holds conference there. If in his barouche, I can see from my window he does not alight, but sits in the vehicle, and Mr. Stanton comes out to attend him.[8] Sometimes one of his sons, a boy of ten or twelve, accompanies him, riding at his right on a pony.

Earlier in the summer I occasionally saw the President and his wife, toward the latter part of the afternoon, out in a barouche, on a pleasure ride through the city. Mrs. Lincoln was dress'd in complete black, with a long crape veil. The equipage is of the plainest kind, only two horses, and they nothing extra. They pass'd me once very close, and I saw the President in the face fully, as they were moving slow, and his look, though abstracted, happen'd to be directed steadily in my eye. He bow'd and smiled, but far beneath his smile I noticed well the expression I have alluded to. None of the artists or pictures have caught the deep, though subtle and indirect expression of this man's face. There is something else there. One of the great portrait painters of two or three centuries ago is needed.[9]

Heated term.

There has lately been much suffering here from heat. We have had it upon us now eleven days. I go around with an umbrella and a fan. I saw two cases of sun-stroke yesterday, one in Pennsylvania avenue, and another in Seventh street. The City Railroad Company loses some horses every day. Yet Washington is having a livelier August, and is probably putting in a more energetic and satisfactory summer, than ever before during its existence. There is probably more human electricity, more population to make it, more business, more light-heartedness, than ever before. The armies that swiftly circumambiated from Fredericksburgh, march'd, struggled, fought, had out their mighty clinch and hurl at Gettysburgh, wheel'd, have circumambiated again, return'd to their ways, touching us not, either at their going or coming. And Washington feels that she has pass'd the worst ; perhaps feels that she is henceforth mistress. So here she sits with her surrounding hills and shores spotted with guns ; and is conscious of a character and identity different from what it was five or six short weeks ago, and very considerably pleasanter and prouder.

Soldiers and Talks.

Soldiers, soldiers, soldiers, you meet everywhere about the city, often superb looking men, though invalids dress'd in worn uniforms, and carrying canes or crutches. I often have talks with them, occasionally quite long and interesting. One, for instance, will have been all through the Peninsula under McClellan—narrates to me the fights, the marches, the strange, quick changes of that eventful campaign, and gives glimpses of many things untold in any official reports or books or journals.[10] These, indeed, are the things that are genuine and precious. The man was there, has been out two years, has been through a dozen fights, the superfluous flesh of talking is long work'd off him, and now he gives me little but the hard meat and sinew.......I find it refreshing, these hardy, bright, intuitive, American young men, (experienced soldiers with all their youth.) The vital play and significance moves one more than books. Then there hangs something majestic about a man who has borne his part in battles, especially if he is very quiet regarding it when you desire him to unbosom. I am continually lost at the absence of blowing and blowers among these old-young American militaires. I have found some man or another who has been in every battle since the War began, and have talk'd with them about each one, in every part of the United States, and many of the engagements on the rivers and harbors too. I find men here from every State in the Union, without exception. (There are more Southerners, especially Border State men, in the Union army than is generally supposed.) I now doubt whether one can get a fair idea of what this War practically is, or what genuine America is, and her character, without some such experience as this I am having.

Death of a Wisconsin Officer.

Another characteristic scene of that dark and bloody 1863, from notes of my visit to Armory Square Hospital, one hot but pleasant summer day. ....In Ward H we approach the cot of a young Lieutenant of one of the Wisconsin regiments. Tread the bare board floor lightly here, for the pain and panting of death are in this cot ! I saw the Lieutenant when he was first brought here from Chancellorsville, and have been with him occasionally from day to day, and night to night. He had been getting along pretty well, till night before last, when a sudden hemorrhage that could not be stopt came upon him, and to-day it still continues at intervals. Notice that water-pail by the side of the bed, with a quantity of blood and bloody pieces of muslin—nearly full ; that tells the story. The poor young man is lying panting, struggling painfully for breath, his great dark eyes with a glaze already upon them, and the choking faint but audible in his throat. An attendant sits by him, and will not leave him till the last ; yet little or nothing can be done. He will die here in an hour or two without the presence of kith or kin. Meantime the ordinary chat and business of the Ward a little way off goes on indifferently. Some of the inmates are laughing and joking, others are playing checkers or cards, others are reading, &c. (I have noticed through most of the hospitals that as long as there is any chance for a man, no matter how bad he may be, the surgeon and nurses work hard, sometimes with curious tenacity, for his life, doing everything, and keeping somebody by him to execute the doctor's orders, and minister to him every minute night and day.........See that screen there. As you advance through the dusk of early candle-light, a nurse will step forth on tip-toe, and silently but imperiously forbid you to make any noise, or perhaps to come near at all. Some soldier's life is flickering there, suspended between recovery and death. Perhaps at this moment the exhausted frame has just fallen into a light sleep that a step might shake. You must retire. The neighboring patients must move in their stocking feet. I have been several times struck with such mark'd efforts—everything bent to save a life from the very grip of the destroyer. But when that grip is once firmly fix'd, leaving no hope or chance at all, the surgeon abandons the patient. If it is a case where stimulus is any relief, the nurse gives milk-punch or brandy, or whatever is wanted, *ad libitum*. There is no fuss made. Not a bit of sentimentalism or whining have I seen about a single death-bed in hospital or on the field, but generally impassive indifference. All is over, as far as any efforts can avail ; it is useless to expend emotions or labors. While there is a prospect they strive hard—at least most surgeons do ; but death certain and evident, they yield the field.)

Aug., Sep., and Oct., '63—The Hospitals.

I am in the habit of going to all, and to Fairfax Seminary, Alexandria, and over Long Bridge to the great Convalescent Camp, &c. The journals publish a regular directory of them—a long list. As a specimen of almost any one of the larger of these Hospitals, fancy to yourself a space of three to twenty acres of ground, on which are group'd ten or twelve very large wooden barracks, with, perhaps, a dozen or twenty, and sometimes more than that number, of small buildings, capable altogether of accommodating from five hundred to a thousand or fifteen hundred persons. Sometimes these wooden barracks or Wards, each of them, perhaps, from a hundred to a hundred and fifty feet long, are ranged in a straight row, evenly fronting the street ; others are plann'd so as to form an immense V ; and others again are ranged around a hollow square. They make altogether a huge cluster, with the additional tents, extra wards for contagious diseases, guard-houses, sutler's stores, chaplain's house, &c. In the middle will probably be an edifice devoted to the offices of the Surgeon in Charge, and the Ward Surgeons, principal attaches, clerks, &c. Then around this centre radiate or are gather'd the Wards for the wounded and sick. The Wards are either letter'd alphabetically, Ward G, Ward K, or else numerically, 1, 2, 3, &c. Each has its Ward Surgeon and corps of nurses. Of course, there is, in the aggregate, quite a muster of employes, and over all the Surgeon in Charge.

The newspaper reader off through the agricultural regions, East or West, sees frequent allusions to these Hospitals, but has probably no clear idea of them. Here in Washington, when they are all fill'd, (as they have been already several times,) they contain a population more numerous in itself than the whole of the Washington of ten or fifteen years ago. Within sight of the Capitol, as I write, are some fifty or sixty such collections or camps, at times holding from fifty to seventy thousand men. Looking from any eminence and studying the topography in my rambles, I use them as landmarks. Through the rich August verdure of the trees see that white group of buildings off yonder in the outskirts ; then another cluster half a mile to the left of the first ; then another a mile to the right, and another a mile beyond, and still another between us and the first. Indeed, we can hardly look in any direction but these grim clusters are dotting the beautiful landscape and environs. That little town, as you might suppose it, off there on the brow of a hill, is indeed a town, but of wounds, sickness, and death. It is Finley Hospital, northeast of the city, on Kendall Green, as it used to be call'd. That other is Campbell Hospital. Both are large establishments. I have known these two alone to have from two thousand to twenty-five hundred inmates. Then there is Carver Hospital, larger still, a wall'd and military city regularly laid out, and guarded by squads of sentries. Again, off east, Lincoln Hospital, a still larger one ; and half a mile further Emory Hospital. Still sweeping the eye around down the river toward Alexandria, we see, to the right, the locality where the Convalescent Camp stands, with its five, eight, or sometimes ten thousand inmates. Even all these are but a portion. The Harewood, Mount Pleasant, Armory Square, Judiciary Hospitals, are some of the rest, already mention'd, and all of them large collections.

Oct. 20.

To-night, after leaving the Hospital, at 10 o'cl'k, (I had been on self-imposed duty some five hours, pretty closely confined,) I wander'd a long time around Washington. The night was sweet, very clear, sufficiently cool, a voluptuous half-moon slightly golden, the space near it of a transparent tinge. I walk'd up Pennsylvania Avenue, and then to Seventh street, and a long while round the Patent Office. Somehow it look'd rebukefully strong, majestic, there in the delicate moonlight. The sky, the planets, the constellations all so bright, so calm, so expressively silent, so soothing, after those Hospital scenes. I wander'd to and fro till the moist moon set, long after midnight.

Spiritual Characters Among the Soldiers.

Every now and then in Hospital or Camp, there are beings I meet—
specimens of unworldliness, disinterestedness and animal purity
and heroism—perhaps some unconscious Indianian, or from Ohio
or Tennessee—on whose birth the calmness of heaven seems to
have descended, and whose gradual growing up, whatever the circumstances of work-life or change, or hardship, or small or no education that attended it, the power of a strange, spiritual sweetness,
fibre and inward health have also attended. Something veil'd and
abstracted is often a part of the manners of these beings. I have met
them, I say, not seldom in the Army, in Camp, and in the great Hospitals. The Western regiments contain many of them. They are
often young men, obeying the events and occasions about them,
marching, soldiering, fighting, foraging, cooking, working on
farms, or at some trade, before the war—unaware of their own
nature, (as to that, who is aware of his own nature?) their companions only understanding that they are different from the rest, more
silent, "something odd about them," and apt to go off and meditate
and muse in solitude.

Cattle Droves About Washington.

Among other sights are immense droves of cattle, with their
drivers, passing through the streets of the city. Some of the men
have a way of leading the cattle on by a peculiar call, a wild, pen-

sive hoot, quite musical, prolong'd, indescribable, sounding something between the coo of a pigeon and the hoot of an owl. I like to stand and look at the sight of one of these immense droves—a little way off—(as the dust is great.) There are always men on horseback, cracking their whips and shouting—the cattle low—some obstinate ox or steer attempts to escape—then a lively scene—the mounted men, always excellent riders and on good horses, dash after the recusant, and wheel and turn—A dozen mounted drovers, their great, slouch'd, broad-brim'd hats, very picturesque—another dozen on foot—everybody cover'd with dust—long goads in their hands—An immense drove of perhaps 2000 cattle—the shouting, hooting, movement, &c.

Hospital Perplexity.

To add to other troubles, amid the confusion of this great army of sick, it is almost impossible for a stranger to find any friend or relative, unless he has the patient's address to start upon. Besides the directory printed in the newspapers here, there are one or two general directories of the Hospitals kept at Provost's headquarters, but they are nothing like complete ; they are never up to date, and, as things are, with the daily streams of coming and going and changing, cannot be. (I have known cases, for instance, such as a farmer coming here from Northern New York to find a wounded brother, faithfully hunting round for a week, and then compell'd to leave and go home without getting any trace of him. When he got home he found a letter from the brother giving the right address in a hospital in Seventh street here.)

CULPEPPER, VA.,
Feb., '64.

Here I am, pretty well down toward the extreme front. Three or four days ago General S., who is now in chief command, (I believe Meade is absent sick,) moved a strong force southward from camp as if intending business. They went to the Rapidan ; there has since been some manouvering and a little fighting, but nothing of consequence. The telegraphic accounts given Monday morning last, make entirely too much of it, I should say. What General S. intended we here know not, but we trust in that competent commander.[11] We were somewhat excited, (but not so very much either,) on Sunday, during the day and night, as orders were sent out to pack up and harness, and be ready to evacuate, to fall back toward Washington. I was very sleepy, and went to bed. Some tremendous shouts arousing me during the night, I went forth and found it was from the men above mention'd, who were returning. I talked with some of the men. As usual I found them full of gayety, endurance, and many fine little outshows, the signs of the most excellent good manliness of the world.......It was a curious sight to see those shadowy columns moving through the night. I stood unobserv'd in the darkness and watch'd them long. The mud was very deep. The men had their usual burdens, overcoats, knapsacks, guns and blankets. Along and along they filed by me, with often a laugh, a song, a cheerful word, but never once a murmur. It may have been odd, but I never before so realized the majesty and reality of the

American common people proper. It fell upon me like a great awe. The strong ranks moved neither fast nor slow. They had march'd seven or eight miles already through the slipping, unctious mud. The brave First Corps stopt here. The equally brave Third Corps moved on to Brandy Station.

The famous Brooklyn 14th are here, guarding the town. You see their red legs actively moving everywhere. Then they have a theatre of their own here. They give musical performances, nearly every thing done capitally. Of course the audience is a jam. It is real good sport to attend one of these entertainments of the 14th. I like to look around at the soldiers, and the general collection of eager and handsome young faces in front of the curtain, more than the scene on the stage.

Paying the Bounties.

One of the things to note here now is the arrival of the paymaster with his strong box, and the payment of bounties to veterans re-enlisting. Major H. is here to-day, with a small mountain of green-backs, rejoicing the hearts of the 2d division of the 1st Corps. In the midst of a ricketty shanty, behind a little table, sit the Major and Clerk Eldridge, with the rolls before them, and much moneys. A re-enlisted man gets in cash about $200 down, (and heavy instalments following, as the pay-days arrive, one after another.) The show of the men crowding around is quite exhilarating. I like well to stand and look. They feel elated, their pockets full, and the ensuing furlough, the visit home. It is a scene of sparkling eyes and flush'd cheeks. The soldier has many gloomy and harsh experiences, and this makes up for some of them. Major H. is order'd to pay first all the re-enlisted men of the 1st Corps their bounties and back pay, and then the rest. You hear the peculiar sound of the rustling of the new and crisp greenbacks by the hour, through the nimble fingers of the Major and my friend Clerk E.[12]

Rumors, Changes, &c.

About the excitement of Sunday, and the orders to be ready to start, I have heard since that the said orders came from some cautious minor commander, and that the high principalities knew not and thought not of any such move ; which is likely. The rumor and fear here intimated a long circuit by Lee, and flank attack on our right. But I cast my eyes at the mud, which was then at its highest and palmiest condition, and retired composedly to rest. Still it is about time for Culpepper to have a change. Authorities have chased each other here like clouds in a stormy sky. Before the first Bull Run this was the rendezvous and camp of instruction of the Secession troops. I am stopping at the house of a lady who has witness'd all the eventful changes of the War, along this route of contending armies. She is a widow, with a family of young children, and lives here with her sister in a large handsome house. A number of army officers board with them.

Virginia.

Dilapidated, fenceless, and trodden with war as Virginia is, wherever I move across her surface, I find myself rous'd to surprise and admiration. What capacity for products, improve-ments, human life, nourishment and expansion ! Everywhere that I have been in the Old Dominion, (the subtle mockery of that title now !) such thoughts have fill'd me. The soil is yet far above the average of any of the northern States. And how full of breadth is the scenery, everywhere with distant mountains, everywhere convenient rivers. Even yet prodigal in forest woods, and surely eligible for all the fruits, orchards, and flow-ers. The skies and atmosphere most luscious, as I feel certain, from more than a year's residence in the State, and movements hither and yon. I should say very healthy, as a general thing. Then a rich and elastic quality, by night and by day. The sun rejoices in his strength, dazzling and burning, and yet, to me, never unpleasantly weakening. It is not the panting tropical heat, but invigorates. The north tempers it. The nights are often unsurpassable. Last evening (Feb. 8,) I saw the first of the new moon, the old moon clear along with it ; the sky and air so clear, such transparent hues of color, it seem'd to me I had never really seen the new moon before. It was the thinnest cut crescent pos-sible. It hung delicate just above the sulky shadow of the Blue Mountains. Ah, if it might prove an omen and good prophecy for this unhappy State.

WASHINGTON
Again — Summer of 1864.

I am back again in Washington, on my regular daily and nightly rounds. Of course there are many specialties. Dotting a Ward here and there are always cases of poor fellows, long-suffering under obstinate wounds, or weak and dishearten'd from typhoid fever, or the like ; mark'd cases, needing special and sympathetic nourishment. These I sit down and either talk to, or silently cheer them up. They always like it hugely, (and so do I.) Each case has its peculiarities, and needs some new adaptation. I have learnt to thus conform—learnt a good deal of hospital wisdom. Some of the poor young chaps, away from home for the first time in their lives, hunger and thirst for affection. This is sometimes the only thing that will reach their condition.......The men like to have a pencil, and something to write in. I have given them cheap pocket-diaries, and almanacs for 1864, interleav'd with blank paper. For reading I generally have some old pictorial magazines or story papers—they are always acceptable. Also the morning or evening papers of the day. The best books I do not give, but *lend* to read through the Wards, and then take them to others, and so on. They are very punctual about returning the books.

In these Wards, or on the field, as I thus continue to go round, I have come to adapt myself to each emergency, after its kind or call, however trivial, however solemn—every one justified and made real under its circumstances—not only visits and cheering talk and little gifts—not only washing and dressing wounds, (I have some cases where the patient is unwilling any one should do this but me)—but passages from the Bible, expounding them, prayer at the bedside, explanations of doctrine, &c. (I think I see my friends smiling at this confession, but I was never more in earnest in my life.)

Readings.

In camp and everywhere, I was in the habit of reading to the men. They were very fond of it, and liked declamatory poetical pieces. We would gather in a large group by ourselves, after supper, and spend the time in such readings, or in talking, and occasionally by an amusing game called the Game of Twenty Questions.

A New Army Organization Fit for America Needed.

It is plain to me out of the events of the War, North and South, and out of all considerations, that the current Military theory, practice, rules and organization, (adopted from Europe from the feudal institutes, with, of course, the "modern improvements," largely from the French,) though tacitly follow'd, and believ'd in by the officers generally, are not at all consonant with the United States, nor our people, nor our days.....What it will be I know not—but I know that as entire an abnegation of the present Military System, (and the Naval too,) and a building up from radically different root-bases and centres appropriate to us, must eventually result, as that our Political system has resulted and become establish'd, different from feudal Europe, and built up on itself from original, perennial, democratic premises.

We have undoubtedly in the United States the greatest Military power—an exhaustless, intelligent, brave and reliable rank and file—in the world, any land, perhaps all lands. The problem is to organize this in the manner fully appropriate to it, to the principles of the Republic, and to get the best service out of it. In the present struggle, as already seen and review'd, probably three-fourths of the losses, men, lives, &c., have been sheer superfluity, extravagance, waste. The body and bulk come out more and more superb—the practical Military system, directing power, crude, illegitimate—worse than deficient, offensive, radically wrong.

Death of a Hero.

I wonder if I could ever convey to another—to you, for instance, Reader dear—the tender and terrible realities of such cases, (many, many happen'd,) as the one I am now going to mention.......Stewart C. Glover, Co. E, Fifth Wisconsin—was wounded, May 5, in one of those fierce tussles of the Wilderness—died May 21—aged about 20. (He was a small and beardless young man—a splendid soldier—in fact, almost an ideal American, of common life, of his age. He had serv'd nearly three years, and would have been entitled to his discharge in a few days. He was in Hancock's Corps.).......The fighting had about ceas'd for the day, and the General commanding the brigade rode by and call'd for volunteers to bring in the wounded. Glover responded among the first—went out gayly—but while in the act of bearing in a wounded sergeant to our lines, was shot in the knee by a rebel sharpshooter. Consequence, amputation and death.......He had resided with his father, John Glover, an aged and feeble man, in Batavia, Genesee Co., N. Y., but was at school in Wisconsin, after the War broke out, and there enlisted—soon took to soldier-life, liked it, was very manly, was belov'd by officers and comrades.......He kept a little diary, like so many of the soldiers. On the day of his death, he wrote the following in it : *To-day, the doctor says I must die — all is over with me — ah, so young to die.* On another blank leaf he pencill'd to his brother, *Dear brother Thomas, I have been brave, but wicked — pray for me.*

A Slight Glimpse.

It is Sunday afternoon, middle of summer, hot and oppressive, and very silent through the Ward. I am taking care of a critical case, now lying in a half lethargy. Near where I sit is a suffering rebel, from the Eighth Louisiana ; his name is Irving. He has been here a long time, badly wounded, and lately had his leg amputated. It is not doing very well. Right opposite me is a sick soldier-boy, laid down with his clothes on, sleeping, looking much wasted, his pallid face on his arm. I see by the yellow trimming on his jacket that he is a cavalry boy. He looks so handsome as he sleeps, one must needs go nearer to him. I step softly over and find by his card that he is named William Cone, of the First Maine Cavalry, and his folks live in Skowhegan.

Ice Cream Treat.

One hot day toward the middle of June, I gave the inmates of Carver Hospital a general ice cream treat, purchasing a large quantity, and, under convoy of the doctor or head nurse of each Ward, going around personally through the Wards to see to its distribution.

An Incident.

In one of the fights before Atlanta, a rebel soldier, of large size, evidently a young man, was mortally wounded in top of the head, so that the brains partially exuded. He lived three days, lying on his back on the spot where he first dropt. He dug with his heel in the ground during that time a hole big enough to put in a couple of ordinary knapsacks. He just lay there in the open air, and with little intermission kept his heel going night and day. Some of our soldiers then moved him to a house, but he died in a few minutes.

Another.

After the battles at Columbia, Tennessee, where we repuls'd about a score of vehement rebel charges, they left a great many wounded on the ground, mostly within our range. Whenever any of these wounded attempted to move away by any means, generally by crawling off, our men without exception, brought them down by a bullet. They let none crawl away, no matter what his condition.

A Yankee Soldier.

As I turn'd off the Avenue one cool October evening into Thirteenth street, a soldier with knapsack and overcoat on, stood at the corner inquiring his way. I found he wanted to go part of the road in my direction, so we walk'd on together. We soon fell into conversation. He was small and not very young, and a tough little fellow, as I judged in the evening light, catching glimpses by the lamps we pass'd. His answers were short, but clear. His name was Charles Carroll ; he belong'd to one of the Massachusetts regiments, and was born in or near Lynn. His parents were living, but were very old. There were four sons, and all had enlisted. Two had died of starvation and misery in the prison at Andersonville, and one had been kill'd in the West. He only was left. He was now going home, and, by the way he talk'd, I inferr'd that his time was nearly out. He made great calculations on being with his parents to comfort them the rest of their days.

Union Prisoners South — Salisbury.

Michael Stansbury, 48 years of age, a sea-faring man, a Southerner by birth and raising, formerly Captain of U.S. light ship Long Shoal, station'd at Long Shoal Point, Pamlico Sound— though a Southerner, a firm Union man—was captur'd Feb. 17, 1863, and has been nearly two years in the Confederate prisons ; was at one time order'd releas'd by Governor Vance, but a rebel officer re-arrested him ; then sent on to Richmond for exchange—but instead of being exchanged was sent down (as a Southern citizen, not a soldier,) to Salisbury, N.C., where he remain'd until lately, when he escaped among the exchanged by assuming the name of a dead soldier, and coming up via Wilmington with the rest. Was about sixteen months in Salisbury. Subsequent to October '64, there were about 11,000 Union pris-

oners in the stockade ; about 100 of them Southern Unionists,
200 U.S. deserters. During the past winter 1500 of the prisoners,
to save their lives, join'd the Confederacy, on condition of being
assign'd merely to guard duty, &c. Out of the 11,000 not more
than 2,500 came out ; 500 of these were pitiable, helpless
wretches—the rest were in a condition to travel. There were
often 60 dead bodies to be buried in the morning ; the daily
average would be about 40. The regular food was a meal of
corn, the cob and husk ground together, and sometimes once a
week a ration of sorghum molasses. A diminutive ration of meat
might possibly come once a month, not oftener....... In the
stockade, containing the 11,000 men, there was a partial show of
tents, (not enough for 2,000.) A large proportion of the men
lived in holes in the ground, in the utmost wretchedness. Some
froze to death, others had their hands and feet frozen. The rebel
guards would occasionally, and on the least pretence, fire into
the prison from mere demonism and wantonness. All the horrors that can be named, cruelty, starvation, lassitude, filth, ver-
min, despair, swift loss of self-respect, idiocy, insanity, and
frequent murder, were there.......Stansbury has a wife and child
living in Newbern—has written to them from here—is in the
U.S. Light House employ still—(had been home to Newbern to
see his family, and on his return to light ship was captured in his
boat.).......Has seen men brought there to Salisbury as hearty as
you ever see in your life—in a few weeks completely dead gone,
much of it from thinking on their condition—hope all
gone.......Has himself a hard, sad, strangely expressive, deaden'd
kind of look, as of one chill'd for years in the cold and dark,
where his good manly nature had no room to exercise itself.

Deserters—Saturday, Oct. 24.

Saw a large squad of our own deserters, (over 300) surrounded with a strong cordon of arm'd guards, marching along Pennsylvania avenue. The most motley collection I ever saw, all sorts of rig, all sorts of hats and caps, many fine-looking young fellows, some of them shame-faced, some sickly, most of them dirty, shirts very dirty and long worn, &c. They tramp'd along without order, a huge huddling mass, not in ranks. I saw some of the spectators laughing, but I felt like anything else but laughing.

These deserters are far more numerous than would be thought. Almost every day I see squads of them, sometimes two or three at a time, with a small guard ; sometimes ten or twelve, under a larger one. (I hear that desertions from the army now in the field have often averaged 10,000 a month. One of the commonest sights in Washington is a squad of deserters. I often think it curious that the military and civil operations do not clash, but they never do here.)[13]

A Glimpse of War's Hell-Scenes.

In one of the late movements of our troops in the Valley, (near Upperville, I think,) a strong force of Moseby's mounted guerillas attack'd a train of wounded, and the guard of cavalry convoying them.[14] The ambulances contain'd about 60 wounded, quite a number of them officers of rank. The rebels were in strength, and the capture of the train and its partial guard after a short snap was effectually accomplish'd.

No sooner had our men surrender'd, the rebels instantly commenced robbing the train, and murdering their prisoners, even the wounded. Here is the scene, or a sample of it, ten minutes after. Among the wounded officers in the ambulances were one, a Lieutenant of regulars, and another of higher rank. These two were dragg'd out on the ground on their backs, and were now surrounded by the guerillas, a demoniac crowd, each member of which was stabbing them in different parts of their bodies. One of the officers had his feet pinn'd firmly to the ground by bayonets stuck through them and thrust into the ground. These two officers, as afterwards found on examination, had receiv'd about twenty such thrusts, some of them through the mouth, face, &c. The wounded had all been dragg'd (to give a better chance also for plunder,) out of their wagons ; some had been effectually dispatch'd, and their bodies lying there lifeless and bloody. Others, not yet dead, but horribly mutilated, were moaning or groaning. Of our men who surrender'd, most had been thus maim'd or slaughter'd.

At this instant a force of our cavalry, who had been following the train at some interval, charged suddenly upon the Secesh captors, who proceeded at once to make the best escape they could. Most of them got away, but we gobbled two officers and seventeen men, as it were in the very acts just described. The sight was one which admitted of little discussion, as may be imagined. The seventeen captured men and two officers were put under guard for the night, but it was decided there and then that they should die.

The next morning the two officers were taken in the town, separate places, put in the centre of the street, and shot. The seventeen men were taken to an open ground, a little to one side. They were placed in a hollow square, encompass'd by two of our cavalry regiments, one of which regiments had three days before found the bloody corpses of three of their men hamstrung and hung up by the heels to limbs of trees by Moseby's guerillas, and the other had not long before had twelve men, after surrendering, shot and then hung by the neck to limbs of trees, and jeering inscriptions pinn'd to the breast of one of the corpses, who had been a sergeant. Those three, and those twelve, had been found, I say, by these environing regiments. Now, with revolvers, they form'd the grim cordon of their seventeen prisoners. The latter were placed in the midst of the hollow square, were unfasten'd, and the ironical remark made to them that they were now to be given "a chance for themselves." A few ran for it. But what use ? From every side the deadly pills came. In a few minutes the seventeen corpses strew'd the hollow square.......I was curious to know whether some of the Union soldiers, some few, (some one or two at least of the youngsters,) did not abstain from shooting on the helpless men. Not one. There was no exultation, very little said ; almost nothing, yet every man there contributed his shot.

(Multiply the above by scores, aye hundreds—varify it in all the forms that different circumstances, individuals, places, &c., could afford—light it with every lurid passion, the wolf's, the lion's lapping thirst for blood, the passionate, boiling volcanoes of human revenge for comrades, brothers slain—with the light of burning farms, and heaps of smutting, smouldering black embers—and in the human heart everywhere black, worse embers—and you have an inkling of this War.)

Gifts—Money—Discrimination.

As a very large proportion of the wounded still come up from the front without a cent of money in their pockets, I soon discover'd that it was about the best thing I could do to raise their spirits, and show them that somebody cared for them, and practically felt a fatherly or brotherly interest in them, to give them small sums, in such cases, using tact and discretion about it. I am regularly supplied with funds for this purpose by good women and men in Boston, Salem, Providence, Brooklyn, and New York. I provide myself with a quantity of bright, new ten-cent and five-cent bills, and, when I think it incumbent, I give 25 or 30 cents, or perhaps 50 cents, and occasionally a still larger sum to some particular case.

As I have recurr'd to this subject several times, I may take opportunity to ventilate and sum up the financial question. My supplies, altogether voluntary, mostly confidential, often seeming quite Providential, were numerous and varied. For instance, there were two distant and wealthy ladies, sisters, who sent regularly, for two years, quite heavy sums, enjoining that their names should be kept secret. The same delicacy was indeed a frequent condition. From several I had *carte blanche*. Many were entire strangers. From these sources, during from two to three years, in the manner described, in the Hospitals, I bestow'd, as almoner for others, many, many thousands of dollars. I learn'd one thing conclusively—that beneath all the ostensible greed and heartlessness of our times there is no end to the generous benevolence of men and women in the United States, when once sure of their object. Another thing became clear to me—while *cash* is not amiss to bring up the rear, tact and magnetic sympathy and unction are, and ever will be, sovereign still.

Items Wanted—(From my Note Books.)

Some of the half-erased and not over-legible when made, memoranda of things wanted, by one patient or another, will convey quite a fair idea. D. S. G. bed 52, wants a good book ; has a sore, weak throat ; would like some horehound candy. Is from New Jersey, 28th regiment.......C. H. L., 145th Pennsylvania, lies in bed 6, with jaundice and erysipelas ; also wounded. Stomach easily nauseated. Bring him some oranges, also a little tart jelly. Hearty, full-blooded young fellow. (He got better in a few days, and is now home on a furlough.).......J. H. G., bed 24, wants an undershirt, drawers and socks. Has not had a change for quite a while. Is evidently a neat clean boy from New England. I supplied him ; also with a comb, tooth-brush, and some soap and towels. I noticed afterward he was the cleanest of the whole

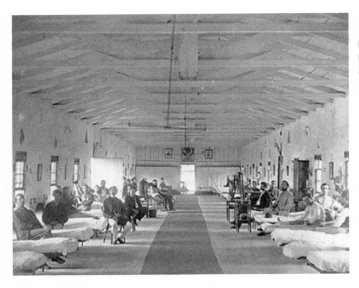

Inside Armory Sqaure Hospital, Washington, D.C., 1865.

Buildings at Armory Square Hospital, with the chapel in the foreground, the Capital in the background.

Surgeons of the 2nd Division, 3rd Corp, at Culpeper, Virginia, in 1863.

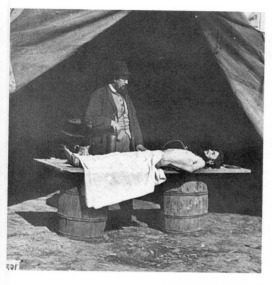

An embalming surgeon at work. Date and location unknown.

Nurses and officers of the United States Sanitary Commission, an official organization whose quality and manner of care for the wounded Whitman did not like. "Incompetent and disagreeable," he called them in a letter to his mother. Taken by James Gardner at Fredericksburg, in May 1864.

The Lacy Mansion, at Falmouth and opposite Fredericksburg, where Whitman first encountered the wounded of the war, in December 1862. Taken by Timothy H. O'Sullivan in March 1863.

The Engineer Corps ambulance train, pictured at Falmouth, Virginia. Taken by Timothy H. O'Sullivan in April 1863.

Winter camp of the Army of the Potomac, at Falmouth. Taken by James F. Gibson in March 1863.

A scene from Harewood Hospital in Washington, D. C.

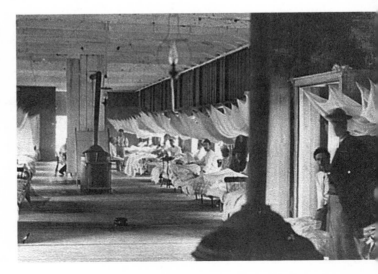

Wounded men from the frightful battle of the Wilderness. Taken by James Gardner at Fredericksburg in May 1864.

Wounded Confederate soldiers from the battle of Antietam. Taken in Maryland by Alexander Gardner, September 1862.

The Federal supply depot at Aquia Creek Landing,
Virginia. Taken by Alexander Gardner in February 1863,
shortly after Whitman's journey there.

Scene from Aquia Creek Landing of the embarkation of
the 9th Army Corps. Taken by Alexander Gardner in
February 1863.

Chicago Public Library
Oriole Park
8/7/2015   1:23:57 PM
-Patron Receipt-

ITEMS BORROWED:

1:
Title: Memoranda during the war /
Item #: R0403152533
Due Date: 8/28/2015

-Please retain for your records-

MBREEN1

Hospital tents behind Douglas Hospital, in
Washington, D. C., taken in May 1864.

Scene from a field hospital during the Peninsular
Campaign, June 1862. Taken at Savage Station, Virginia
by James F. Gibson.

Douglas Hospital, in Washington, D. C., front and side view. Taken in May 1864.

Portrait of surgeons from the 3rd Division, at Petersburg, Virginia. Taken in August 1864, during the siege of Petersburg.

Washington, D.C., office of the U.S. Christian Commission. Taken in April 1865.

Walt Whitman's letter to Mr. and Mrs. Haskell, July 27, 1863.

Washington
July 27 1863

Mr & Mrs Haskell
     Your son Erastus
Haskell, of co K 141st
New York, is now lying
sick with typhoid fever
here in hospital.
     I have
been quite
                 was with
for a few day,
much inter
young man
been very
to be so
Should jud

Walt Whitman
Soldiers
Missionary
     to Hospital, Camp, & Battle Ground
(Young Men's Christian Commission
343 Pennsylvania av. Washington
                                                    D.C.)

Office at Mayor   paymaster
cor 15th
telegraph 394 L st near 14th
                              Washington

(Residence, Brooklyn N.Y.
     Portland av. near Myrtle

"Walt Whitman, Soldier's Missionary to Hospital, Camp, and Battle Ground." Whitman's war notebook from 1863.

Richard Hunt, 68 Stanton st. 2d av. car
Rebecca Velson 130 Suffolk st.
Robley 18th st. & 9th av. Gowanus.
H. Peters, cor Cherry st. & Franklin sq.
Herman Storms, Pascack p.o. Bergen co. N.J.
Noah Hanford Pelham, (Hants)
Thos. P. Nichols 69 Carlton av.
Wm Metzler, Tiskilwa, Bureau co. Illinois
Mrs. Harriet Erwin, (Saml. Erwin)
         Malone, Franklin co. N.Y.

Robertson M. Bryant.

Silas S. Soule, Lieut. 1st Colorado Volunteers.

Albert Jones, (Cack Jones' son)

Frank, (Beeswax.)

Jack Campbell, E. Brooklyn. formerly policeman, now carpenter.

George Applegate, (allest — Dan Applegate.
Wm Phillips, large, light comp. met in '56 or '7 in ale house
        in Myrtle av. near Pearl — afterward told me he was
        living out in Jersey, — belonged to No. 8 engine
James, (oldest) and John Rose. ('5-7.) Classon av.

John Stoothoff, policeman, (blonde) Fulton st.

Charles Held.
Felix McClusky, (fine California — red hair)
Wm Culver, boy in bath, aged 18. (gone to California '56.
Tom Egbert, conductor Myrtle av. open neck, sailor looking
Robert, (Dad.) 23d st.

Edmund Bryant—elder } sons of Dr. Bryant.
Melville   "   Northport. L.I.
Charles Quail, policeman N.Y.
David Stewart, No 12. E. Brooklyn
Abe Delevoise   (Dave Ackerman (bones)
Joe   Broadway & 42d
Johnny Nevin.
Mike Butler, stone cutter, Kent av.
Martin Evans, }
Norris   "   }   (George Wright
                            plasterer
Martha, in Burroughs's saloon
Sam.   (sons bellow. I met at Dominick Colgan's
              plumber)
Tom Lambert, tall, mason, black-eyed
David Barnet, (elder)
Egan   (younger
Elisha "Bill, & Dave Jones, (4th av.)
Elias B. Pierson } sailor
John   "   } gone soldiers

Lincoln
H. H. Brigham 21st Mass
Lincoln
Valentine Fisher F 51st N.Y.
armory
Danl Johnson B. 51st Penn
mt
pleasant John Hall. F. 51st N.Y.
Finly Corp Frederick Sanders k 51st N Y
  " Eugene Dilley H
  " Jas Cremer H
  " Serg Jas C Brown A
  " Sergt John E Gibbs H
  " John Gafney G
  " Ephraim S Warden D
Campbell Jas O'Neil G
  " John Huber B

Judiciary
Mark Deary c 51st Penn

(Harewood)
Wm Cohen B 21st Mass
P J Dixon B 21st Mass

A page from Whitman's later hospital notebook, from 1864.

OPPOSITE: A page from Whitman's "1862" notebook, with his characteristic listing of names.

Ward.......Mrs. G., lady nurse, Ward F., wants a bottle of brandy—has two patients imperatively requiring stimulus—low with wounds and exhaustion. (I supplied her with a bottle of first-rate brandy, from the Christian Commission rooms.)

A Case from Second Bull Run.

Well, poor John Mahay is dead. He died yesterday. His was a painful and long lingering case, [see Wednesday, Feb. 4th, pp. 15–16] I have been with him at times for the past fifteen months. He belonged to Company A, One Hundred and First New York, and was shot through the lower region of the abdomen at second Bull Run, August, '62. One scene at his bedside will suffice for the agonies of nearly two years. The bladder had been perforated by a bullet going entirely through him. Not long since I sat a good part of the morning by his bedside, Ward E, Armory Square. The water ran out of his eyes from the intense pain, and the muscles of his face were distorted, but he utter'd nothing except a low groan now and then. Hot moist cloths were applied, and reliev'd him somewhat. Poor Mahay, a mere boy in age, but old in misfortune. He never knew the love of parents, was placed in his infancy in one of the New York charitable institutions, and subsequently bound out to a tyrannical master in Sullivan County, (the scars of whose cowhide and club remain'd yet on his back.) His wound here was a most disagreeable one, for he was a gentle, cleanly and affectionate boy. He found friends in his hospital life, and, indeed, was a universal favorite. He had quite a funeral ceremony.

Army Surgeons—Aid deficiencies.

I must bear my most emphatic testimony to the zeal, manliness, and professional spirit and capacity, generally prevailing among the Surgeons, many of them young men, in the Hospitals and the army. I will not say much about the exceptions, for they are few ; (but I have met some of those few, and very incompetent and airish they were.) I never ceas'd to find the best young men, and the hardest and most disinterested workers, among these Surgeons, in the Hospitals. They are full of genius, too. I have seen many hundreds of them, and this is my testimony.

There are, however, serious deficiencies, wastes, sad want of system, &c., in the Commissions, contributions, and in all the Voluntary, and a great part of the Governmental, nursing, edibles, medicines, stores, &c. (I do not say surgical attendance, because the Surgeons cannot do more than human endurance permits.) Whatever puffing accounts there may be in the papers of the North, this is the actual fact. No thorough previous preparation, no system, no foresight, no genius. Always plenty of stores, no doubt, but always miles away ; never where they are needed, and never the proper application. Of all harrowing experiences, none is greater than that of the days following a heavy battle. Scores, hundreds of the noblest young men on earth, uncomplaining, lie, helpless, mangled, faint, alone, and so bleed to death, or die from exhaustion, either actually untouch'd at all, or merely the laying of them down and leaving them, when there ought to be means provided to save them.

The Blue Everywhere.

This city, its suburbs, the Capitol, the front of the White House, the places of amusement, the Avenue, and all the main streets, swarm with soldiers this winter more than ever before. Some are out from the Hospitals, some from the neighboring camps, &c. One source or another, they pour in plenteously, and make, I should say, the mark'd feature in the human movement and costume-appearance of our National city. Their blue pants and over-coats are everywhere. The clump of crutches is heard, and up the stairs of the Paymasters' offices ; and there are characteristic groups around the doors of the same, often waiting long and wearily in the cold.......Toward the latter part of the afternoon you see the fur-lough'd men, sometimes singly, sometimes in small squads, making their way to the Baltimore depot. At all times, except early in the morning, the patrol detachments are moving around, especially during the earlier hours of evening, examining passes, and arresting all without them. They do not question the one-legged, or men badly disabled or maim'd, but all others are stopt. They also go around through the auditoriums of the theatres, and make officers and all show their passes, or other authority, for being there.

Sunday, Jan. 29, 1865.

Have been in Armory Square this afternoon.[15] The Wards are very comfortable, with new floors and plaster walls, and models of neatness. I am not sure but this is a model hospital after all, in important respects. I found several sad cases of old, lingering wounds. One Delaware soldier, Wm. H. Millis, from Bridgeville, whom I had been with after the battles of the Wilderness, last May, where he receiv'd a very bad wound in the chest, with another in the left arm, and whose case was serious (pneumonia had set in) all last June and July, I now find well enough to do light duty. For three weeks at the time mention'd, he just hover'd between life and death.

Boys in the Army.

As I walk'd home about sunset, I saw in Fourteenth street a very young soldier, thinly clad, standing near the house I was about to enter. I stopt a moment in front of the door and call'd him to me. I knew that an old Tennessee Union regiment, and also an Indiana regiment, were temporarily stopping in new barracks, near Fourteenth street. This boy I found belonged to the Tennessee regiment. But I could hardly believe he carried a musket. He was but 15 years old, yet had been twelve months a soldier, and had borne his part in several battles, even historic ones.......I ask'd him if he did not suffer from the cold and if he had no overcoat. No, he did not suffer from cold, and had no overcoat, but could draw one whenever he wish'd. His father was dead, and his mother living in some part of East Tennessee ; all the men were from that part of the country.

The next forenoon I saw the Tennessee and Indiana regiments marching down the Avenue. My boy was with the former, stepping along with the rest. There were many other boys no older. I stood and watch'd them as they tramp'd along with slow, strong, heavy, regular steps. There did not appear to be a man over 30 years of age, and a large proportion were from 15 to perhaps 22 or 23. They had all the look of veterans, worn, stain'd, impassive, and a certain unbent, lounging gait, carrying in addition to their regular arms and knapsacks, frequently a frying-pan, broom, &c. They were all of pleasant, even handsome physiognomy ; no refinement, nor blanch'd with intellect, but as my eye pick'd them, moving along, rank by rank, there did not seem to be a single repulsive, brutal or markedly stupid face among them.

Burial of a Lady Nurse.

Here is an incident that has just occurr'd in one of the Hospitals. A lady named Miss or Mrs. Billings, who has long been a practical friend of soldiers and nurse in the army, and had become attach'd to it in a way that no one can realize but him or her who has had experience, was taken sick, early this winter, linger'd some time, and finally died in the Hospital. It was her request that she should be buried among the soldiers, and after the military method. This request was fully carried out. Her coffin was carried to the grave by soldiers, with the usual escort, buried, and a salute fired over the grave. This was at Annapolis a few days since.

Female Nurses for Soldiers.

There are many women in one position or another, among the Hospitals, mostly as nurses here in Washington, and among the military stations ; quite a number of them young ladies acting as volunteers. They are a great help in certain ways, and deserve to be mention'd with praise and respect. Then it remains to be distinctly said that few or no young ladies, under the irresistible conventions of society, answer the practical requirements of nurses for soldiers. Middle-aged or healthy and good condition'd elderly women, mothers of children, are always best. Many of the wounded must be handled. A hundred things which cannot be gainsay'd, must occur and must be done. The presence of a good middle-aged or elderly woman, the magnetic touch of hands, the expressive features of the mother, the silent soothing of her presence, her words, her knowledge and privileges arrived at only through having had children, are precious and final qualifications. (Mrs. H. J. Wright, of Mansion House Hospital, Alexandria, is one of those good nurses. I have known her for over two years in her labors of love.) It is a natural faculty that is required ; it is not merely having a genteel young woman at a table in a Ward. One of the finest nurses I met was a red-faced illiterate old Irish woman ; I have seen her take the poor wasted naked boys so tenderly up in her arms. There are plenty of excellent clean old black women that would make tip-top nurses.

Southern Escapees, Feb. 23, '65.

I saw a large procession of young men from the rebel army, (deserters they are call'd, but the usual meaning of the word does not apply to them,) passing along the Avenue to-day.[16] There were nearly 200 of them, come up yesterday by boat from James River. I stood and watch'd them as they pass'd along in a slow, tired, worn sort of way. There was a curiously large proportion of light-hair'd, blonde, light gray-eyed young men among them. Their costumes had a dirt-stain'd uniformity ; most had been originally gray ; some among them had articles of our uniform, pants on one, vest or coat on another. I think they were mostly Georgia and North Carolina boys. They excited little or no attention. As I stood quite close to them, several good looking enough American youths, (but O what a tale of misery their appearance told,) nodded or just spoke to me, without doubt divining pity and fatherliness out of my face, for my heart was full enough of it. Several of the couples trudged along with their arms about each other, some probably brothers ; it seem'd as if they were afraid they might some how get separated. They nearly all look'd what one might call simple, yet intelligent enough, too. Some had pieces of old carpet, some blankets, and others old bags around their shoulders, and some of them here and there had fine faces, still it was a procession of misery. The two hundred had with them about half a dozen arm'd guards.

Along this week I saw some such procession, more or less in

numbers, every day, as they were brought up by the boat. The Government does what it can for them, and sends them North and West.

Feb. 27, '65.

Some three or four hundred more escapees from the Confederate army came up on the boat to-day. As the day has been very pleasant indeed, (after a long spell of bad weather,) I have been wandering around a good deal, without any other object than to be out-doors and enjoy it ; have met these escaped men in all directions. Their apparel is the same ragged, long-worn motley as before described. I talk'd with a number of the men. Some are quite bright and stylish, for all their poor clothes—walking with an air, wearing their old head-coverings on one side, quite saucily. (I find the old, unquestionable proofs, as all along, the past four years, of the unscrupulous tyranny exercised by the Secession government in conscripting the common people by absolute force everywhere, and paying no attention whatever to the men's time being up—keeping them in military service just the same.).......One gigantic young fellow, a Georgian, at least six feet three inches high, broad-sized in proportion, attired in the dirtiest, drab, well-smear'd rags, tied with strings, his trousers at the knees all strips and streamers, was complacently standing eating some bread and meat. He appear'd contented enough. Then a few minutes after I saw him slowly walking along. It was plain he did not take anything to heart.

Feb. 28.

As I pass'd the military headquarters of the city, not far from the President's house, I stopt to talk with some of the crowd of escapees who were lounging there. In appearance they were the same as previously mention'd. Two of them, one about 17, and the other perhaps 25 or 6, I talk'd with some time. They were from North Carolina, born and rais'd there, and had folks there. The elder had been in the rebel service four years. He was first conscripted for two years. He was then kept arbitrarily in the ranks. This is the case with a large proportion of the Secession army. There is no shame in leaving such service—was nothing downcast in these young men's manners. The younger had been soldiering about a year. He was conscripted. There were six brothers (all the boys of the family) in the army, part of them as conscripts, part as volunteers. Three had been kill'd. One had escaped about four months ago, and now this one had got away. He was a pleasant and well-talking lad, with the peculiar North Carolina idiom, (not at all disagreeable to my ears.) He and the elder one were of the same company, and escaped together—and wish'd to remain together. They thought of getting transportation away to Missouri, and working there ; but were not sure it was judicious. I advised them rather to go to some of the directly northern States, and get farm work for the present. The younger had made six dollars on the boat, with some tobacco he brought ; he had three and a half left. The elder had nothing. I gave him a trifle.......Soon after, I met John Wormley, 9th Alabama—is a

West Tennessee rais'd boy, parents both dead—had the look of one for a long time on short allowance—said very little—chew'd tobacco at a fearful rate, spitting in proportion—large clear dark-brown eyes, very fine—didn't know what to make of me—told me at last he wanted much to get some clean underclothes, and a pair of decent pants. Didn't care about coat or hat fixings. Wanted a chance to wash himself well, and put on the under-clothes. I had the very great pleasure of helping him to accomplish all those wholesome designs.

March 1st.

Plenty more butternut or clay-color'd escapees every day. About 160 came in to-day, a large portion South Carolinians. They generally take the oath of allegiance, and are sent north, west, or extreme south-west if they wish. Several of them told me that the desertions in their army, of men going home, leave or no leave, are far more numerous than their desertions to our side. I saw a very forlorn looking squad of about a hundred, late this afternoon, on their way to the Baltimore depot.

To-night I have been wandering awhile in the Capitol, which is all lit up. The illuminated Rotunda looks fine. I like to stand aside and look a long, long while, up at the dome ; it comforts me somehow. The House and Senate were both in session till very late. I look'd in upon them, but only a few moments ; they were hard at work on tax and appropriation bills. I wander'd through the long and rich corridors and apartments under the Senate ; an old habit of mine, former winters, and now more satisfaction than ever. Not many persons down there, occasionally a flitting figure in the distance.

The Inauguration, March 4.[17]

The President very quietly rode down to the Capitol in his own carriage, by himself, on a sharp trot, about noon, either because he wish'd to be on hand to sign bills, &c., or to get rid of marching in line with the absurd procession, the muslin Temple of Liberty, and pasteboard Monitor. I saw him on his return, at three o'clock, after the performance was over. He was in his plain two-horse barouche, and look'd very much worn and tired ; the lines, indeed, of vast responsibilites, intricate questions, and demands of life and death, cut deeper than ever upon his dark brown face ; yet all the old goodness, tenderness, sadness, and canny shrewdness, underneath the furrows. (I never see that man without feeling that he is one to become personally attach'd to, for his combination of purest, heartiest tenderness, and native Western even rudest forms of manliness.) By his side sat his little boy, of ten years. There were no soldiers, only a lot of civilians on horseback, with huge yellow scarfs over their shoulders, riding around the carriage. (At the Inauguration four years ago, he rode down and back again, surrounded by a dense mass of arm'd cavalrymen eight deep, with drawn sabres ; and there were sharp-shooters station'd at every corner on the route.)

I ought to make mention of the closing Levee of Saturday night last. Never before was such a compact jam in front of the White House—all the grounds fill'd, and away out to the spacious sidewalks.......I was there, as I took a notion to go—was in the rush inside with the crowd—surged along the passage-ways, the Blue and other rooms, and through the great East room, (upholster'd like a stage parlor.) Crowds of country people, some very funny. Fine music from the Marine Band, off in a side place.......I saw Mr. Lincoln, drest all in black, with white kid gloves, and a claw-hammer coat, receiving, as in duty bound, shaking hands, looking very disconsolate, and as if he would give anything to be somewhere else.

The Weather—Does it Sympathise with these Times ?

Whether the rains, the heat and cold, and what underlies them all, are affected with what affects man in masses, and follow his play of passionate action, strain'd stronger than usual, and on a larger scale than usual—whether this, or no, it is certain that there is now, and has been for twenty months or more on this American Continent North, many a remarkable, many an unprecedented expression of the subtile world of air above us and around us. There, since this War, and the wide and deep National agitation, strange analogies, different combinations, a different sunlight, or absence of it ; different products even out of the ground. After every great battle, a great storm. Even civic events, the same. On Saturday last, a forenoon like whirling demons, dark, with slanting rain, full of rage ; and then the afternoon, so calm, so bathed with flooding splendor from heaven's most excellent sun, with atmosphere of sweetness ; so clear, it show'd the stars, long, long before they were due. As the Presi-

dent came out on the Capitol portico, a curious little white
cloud, the only one in that part of the sky, appear'd like a hovering bird, right over him.

Indeed, the heavens, the elements, all the meteorological
influences, have run riot for weeks past. Such caprices, abruptest
alternation of frowns and beauty, I never knew. It is a common
remark that (as last Summer was different in its spells of intense
heat from any preceding it,) the Winter just completed has been
without parallel. It has remain'd so down to the hour I am writing. Much of the day-time of the past month was sulky, with
leaden heaviness, fog, interstices of bitter cold, and some insane
storms. But there have been samples of another description. Nor
earth, nor sky ever knew spectacles of superber beauty than some
of the nights have lately been here. The western star, Venus, in
the earlier hours of evening, has never been so large, so clear ; it
seems as if it told something, as if it held rapport indulgent with
humanity, with us Americans. Five or six nights since, it hung
close by the moon, then a little past its first quarter. The star was
wonderful, the moon like a young mother. The sky, dark blue,
the transparent night, the planets, the moderate west wind, the
elastic temperature, the unsurpassable miracle of that great star,
and the young and swelling moon swimming in the west, suf-
fused the soul. Then I heard, slow and clear, the deliberate notes
of a bugle come up out of the silence, sounding so good
through the night's mystery, no hurry, but firm and faithful,
floating along, rising, falling leisurely, with here and there a
long-drawn note ; the bugle, well play'd, sounding tattoo, in
one of the army Hospitals near here, where the wounded (some
of them personally so dear to me,) are lying in their cots, and

many a sick boy come down to the war from Illinois, Michigan, Wisconsin, Iowa, and the rest.

March 6—Inauguration Ball.

I have this moment been up to look at the gorgeous array'd dance and supper-rooms, for the Inauguration Ball, at the Patent Office, (which begins in a few hours ;) and I could not help thinking of those rooms, where the music will sound and the dancers' feet presently tread—what a different scene they presented to my view a while since, fill'd with a crowded mass of the worst wounded of the war, brought in from Second Bull Run, Antietam and Fredericks-burgh. To-night, beautiful women, perfumes, the violins' sweet-ness, the polka and the waltz ; but then, the amputation, the blue face, the groan, the glassy eye of the dying, the clotted rag, the odor of wounds and blood, and many a mother's son amid strangers, passing away untended there, (for the crowd of the badly hurt was great, and much for nurse to do, and much for surgeon.)

Scene at the Capitol.

I must mention a strange scene at the Capitol, the Hall of Repre-sentatives, the morning of Saturday last, (March 4th.) The day just dawn'd, but in half-darkness, everything dim, leaden, and soaking. In that dim light the members nervous from long drawn duty, exhausted, some asleep, and many half asleep. The gas-light, mix'd with the dingy day-break, produced an unearthly effect. The poor little sleepy, stumbling pages, the smell of the Hall, the members with heads leaning on their desks asleep, the sounds of the voices speaking, with unusual intonations—the general moral atmosphere also of the close of this important session—the strong hope that the War is approaching its close—the tantalizing dread lest the hope may be a false one—the grandeur of the Hall itself, with its effect of vast shadows up toward the panels and spaces over the galleries—all made a mark'd combination.

In the midst of this, with the suddenness of a thunderbolt, burst one of the most angry and crashing storms of rain and wind ever heard. It beat like a deluge on the heavy glass roof of the Hall, and the wind literally howl'd and roar'd. For a moment, (and no wonder,) the nervous and sleeping Representatives were thrown into confusion. The slumberers awaked with fear, some started for the doors, some look'd up with blanch'd cheeks and lips to the roof, and the little pages began to cry ; it was a scene ! But it was over almost as soon as the drowsied men were actually awake. They recover'd themselves ; the storm raged on, beating, dashing, and with loud noises at times. But the House went ahead with its business then, I think, as calmly and with as much deliberation as at any time in its career. Perhaps the shock did it good. (One is not without impression, after all, amid these members of Congress, of both the Houses, that if the flat and selfish routine of their duties should ever be broken in upon by some great emergency involving real danger, and calling for first-class personal qualities, those qualities would be found generally forthcoming, and from men not now credited with them.)

March 27, 1865—A Yankee Antique.

Sergeant Calvin F. Harlowe, Co. C, Twenty-Ninth Massachusetts, Third Brigade, First Division, Ninth Corps—a mark'd
sample of heroism and death, (some may say bravado, but I say
heroism, of grandest, oldest order)—in the late attack by the
rebel troops, and temporary capture by them, of Fort Steadman,
at night. The Fort was surprised at dead of night. Suddenly
awaken'd from their sleep, and rushing from their tents, Harlowe, with others, found himself in the hands of the Secesh—
they demanded his surrender—he answer'd, *Never while I live.*
(Of course it was useless. The others surrender'd ; the odds were
too great.) Again he was ask'd to yield, this time by a rebel Captain. Though surrounded, and quite calm, he again refused,
call'd sternly to his comrades to fight on, and himself attempted to
do so. The rebel Captain then shot him—but at the same instant
he shot the Captain. Both fell together, mortally wounded. Harlowe died almost instantly. (The rebels were driven out in a very
short time.) The body was buried next day, but soon taken up and
sent home, (Plymouth Co., Mass.).......Harlowe was only 22 years
of age—was a tall, slim, dark-hair'd, blue-eyed young man—had
come out originally with the Twenty-Ninth Mass., and that is the
way he met his death, after four years campaign. He was in the
Seven Days Fight before Richmond, Second Bull Run, Antietam,
First Fredericksburgh, Vicksburgh, Jackson, Wilderness, and the
campaigns following—was as good a soldier as ever wore the blue,
and every old officer of the regiment will bear that testi-

mony........Though so young, and in a common rank, he had a spirit as resolute and brave as any hero in the books, ancient or modern—It was too great to say the words "I surrender"—and so he died.......(When I think of such things, knowing them well, all the vast and complicated events of the War on which History dwells and makes its volumes, fall indeed aside, and for the moment at any rate I see nothing but young Calvin Harlowe's figure in the night disdaining to surrender.)

Wounds and Diseases.

The war is over, but the hospitals are fuller than ever, from former and current cases. A large majority of the wounds are in the arms and legs. But there is every kind of wound, in every part of the body. I should say of the sick, from my observation, that the prevailing maladies are typhoid fever and the camp fevers generally, diarrhoea, catarrhal affections and bronchitis, rheumatism and pneumonia. These forms of sickness lead ; all the rest follow. There are twice as many sick as there are wounded. The deaths range from 7 to 10 per cent. of those under treatment.

Murder of President Lincoln.[18]

The day, April 14, 1865, seems to have been a pleasant one throughout the whole land—the moral atmosphere pleasant too—the long storm, so dark, so fratricidal, full of blood and doubt and gloom, over and ended at last by the sun-rise of such

an absolute National victory, and utter breaking-down of Secessionism—we almost doubted our own senses ! Lee had capitulated beneath the apple-tree of Appomattax. The other armies,
the flanges of the revolt, swiftly follow'd.......And could it really
be, then ? Out of all the affairs of this world of woe and passion,
of failure and disorder and dismay, was there really come the
confirm'd, unerring sign of plan, like a shaft of pure light—of
rightful rule—of God ?.......So the day, as I say, was propitious.
Early herbage, early flowers, were out. (I remember where I was
stopping at the time, the season being advanced, there were
many lilacs in full bloom. By one of those caprices that enter and
give tinge to events without being at all a part of them, I find
myself always reminded of the great tragedy of that day by the
sight and odor of these blossoms. It never fails.)

But I must not dwell on accessories. The deed hastens. The
popular afternoon paper of Washington, the little *Evening Star,*
had spatter'd all over its third page, divided among the advertisements in a sensational manner in a hundred different places, *The
President and his Lady will be at the Theatre this evening*.......(Lincoln was fond of the theatre. I have myself seen him there several
times. I remember thinking how funny it was that He, in some
respects, the leading actor in the greatest and stormiest drama
known to real history's stage, through centuries, should sit there
and be so completely interested and absorb'd in those human
jack-straws, moving about with their silly little gestures, foreign
spirit, and flatulent text.)

On this occasion the theatre was crowded, many ladies in rich
and gay costumes, officers in their uniforms, many well known
citizens, young folks, the usual clusters of gaslights, the usual

magnetism of so many people, cheerful, with perfumes, music of violins and flutes—(and over all, and saturating all, that vast vague wonder, *Victory,* the Nation's Victory, the triumph of the Union, filling the air, the thought, the sense, with exhilaration more than all perfumes.)

The President came betimes, and, with his wife, witness'd the play, from the large stage-boxes of the second tier, two thrown into one, and profusely draped with the National flag. The acts and scenes of the piece—one of those singularly witless[19] compositions which have at least the merit of giving entire relief to an audience engaged in mental action or business excitements and cares during the day, as it makes not the slightest call on either the moral, emotional, esthetic, or spiritual nature—a piece, ('Our American Cousin,') in which, among other characters, so call'd, a Yankee, certainly such a one as was never seen, or the least like it ever seen, in North America, is introduced in England, with a varied fol-de-rol of talk, plot, scenery, and such phantasmagoria as goes to make up a modern popular drama— had progress'd through perhaps a couple of its acts, when in the midst of this comedy, or tragedy, or non-such, or whatever it is to be call'd, and to off-set it or finish it out, as if in Nature's and the Great Muse's mockery of those poor mimes, comes interpolated that Scene, not really or exactly to be described at all, (for on the many hundreds who were there it seems to this hour to have left little but a passing blur, a dream, a blotch)—and yet partially to be described as I now proceed to give it.......There is a scene in the play representing a modern parlor, in which two unprecedented English ladies are inform'd by the unprecedented and impossible Yankee that he is not a man of fortune, and

therefore undesirable for marriage-catching purposes ; after
which, the comments being finish'd, the dramatic trio make exit,
leaving the stage clear for a moment. There was a pause, a hush
as it were. At this period came the murder of Abraham Lincoln.
Great as that was, with all its manifold train, circling round it,
and stretching into the future for many a century, in the politics,
history, art, &c., of the New World, in point of fact the main
thing, the actual murder, transpired with the quiet and simplicity of any commonest occurrence—the bursting of a bud or pod
in the growth of vegetation, for instance. Through the general
hum following the stage pause, with the change of positions,
&c., came the muffled sound of a pistol shot, which not one
hundredth part of the audience heard at the time—and yet a
moment's hush—somehow, surely a vague startled thrill—and
then, through the ornamented, draperied, starr'd and striped
space-way of the President's box, a sudden figure, a man raises
himself with hands and feet, stands a moment on the railing,
leaps below to the stage, (a distance of perhaps fourteen or fifteen feet,) falls out of position, catching his boot-heel in the
copious drapery, (the American flag,) falls on one knee, quickly
recovers himself, rises as if nothing had happen'd, (he really
sprains his ankle, but unfelt then,)—and so the figure, Booth,
the murderer, dress'd in plain black broadcloth, bare-headed,
with a full head of glossy, raven hair, and his eyes like some mad
animal's flashing with light and resolution, yet with a certain
strange calmness, holds aloft in one hand a large knife—walks
along not much back from the footlights—turns fully toward
the audience his face of statuesque beauty, lit by those basilisk
eyes, flashing with desperation, perhaps insanity—launches out

in a firm and steady voice the words, *Sic semper tyrannis*—and then walks with neither slow nor very rapid pace diagonally across to the back of the stage, and disappears.......(Had not all this terrible scene—making the mimic ones preposterous—had it not all been rehears'd, in blank, by Booth, beforehand?)

A moment's hush, incredulous—a scream—the cry of *Murder*—Mrs. Lincoln leaning out of the box, with ashy cheeks and lips, with involuntary cry, pointing to the retreating figure, *He has kill'd the President*.......And still a moment's strange, incredulous suspense—and then the deluge!—then that mixture of horror, noises, uncertainty—(the sound, somewhere back, of a horse's hoofs clattering with speed)—the people burst through chairs and railings, and break them up—that noise adds to the queerness of the scene—there is inextricable confusion and terror—women faint—quite feeble persons fall, and are trampled on—many cries of agony are heard—the broad stage suddenly fills to suffocation with a dense and motley crowd, like some horrible carnival—the audience rush generally upon it—at least the strong men do—the actors and actresses are all there in their play-costumes and painted faces, with mortal fright showing through the rouge, some trembling—some in tears—the screams and calls, confused talk—redoubled, trebled—two or three manage to pass up water from the stage to the President's box—others try to clamber up—&c., &c., &c.

In the midst of all this, the soldiers of the President's Guard, with others, suddenly drawn to the scene, burst in—(some two hundred altogether)—they storm the house, through all the tiers, especially the upper ones, inflamed with fury, literally charging the audience with fix'd bayonets, muskets and pistols, shouting *Clear out ! clear out ! you sons of*——.......Such the wild scene, or a suggestion of it rather, inside the play-house that night.

Outside, too, in the atmosphere of shock and craze, crowds of people, fill'd with frenzy, ready to seize any outlet for it, come near committing murder several times on innocent individuals. One such case was especially exciting. The infuriated crowd, through some chance, got started against one man, either for words he utter'd, or perhaps without any cause at all, and were proceeding at once to actually hang him on a neighboring lamp post, when he was rescued by a few heroic policemen, who placed him in their midst and fought their way slowly and amid great peril toward the Station House.......It was a fitting episode of the whole affair. The crowd rushing and eddying to and fro — the night, the yells, the pale faces, many frighten'd people trying in vain to extricate themselves — the attack'd man, not yet freed from the jaws of death, looking like a corpse — the silent resolute half-dozen policemen, with no weapons but their little clubs, yet stern and steady through all those eddying swarms — made indeed a fitting side-scene to the grand tragedy of the murder.......They gain'd the Station House with the protected man, whom they placed in security for the night, and discharged him in the morning.

And in the midst of that night-pandemonium of senseless hate, infuriated soldiers, the audience and the crowd — the stage, and all its actors and actresses, its paint-pots, spangles, and gas-lights — the life-blood from those veins, the best and sweetest of the land, drips slowly down, and death's ooze already begins its little bubbles on the lips.......Such, hurriedly sketch'd, were the accompaniments of the death of President Lincoln. So suddenly and in murder and horror unsurpass'd he was taken from us. But his death was painless.

[He leaves for America's History and Biography, so far, not only its most dramatic reminiscence—he leaves, in my opinion, the greatest, best, most characteristic, artistic, Personality. Not but that he had faults, and show'd them in the Presidency ; but honesty, goodness, shrewdness, conscience, and (a new virtue, unknown to other lands, and hardly yet really known here, but the foundation and tie of all, as the future will grandly develop,) Unionism, in its truest and amplest sense, form'd the hard-pan of his character. These he seal'd with his life. The tragic splendor of his death, purging, illuminating all, throws round his form, his head, an aureole that will remain and will grow brighter through time, while History lives, and love of Country lasts. By many has *this Union* been conserv'd and help'd ; but if one name, one man, must be pick'd out, he, most of all, is the Conservator of it, to the future. He was assassinated—but the Union is not assassinated—*ça ira* ! One falls, and another falls. The soldier drops, sinks like a wave— but the ranks of the ocean eternally press on. Death does its work, obliterates a hundred, a thousand—President, general, captain, private—but the Nation is immortal.]

Releas'd Union Prisoners from South.

The releas'd prisoners of War are now coming up from the Southern prisons. I have seen a number of them. The sight is worse than any sight of battle-fields or any collections of wounded, even the bloodiest. There was, (as a sample,) one large boat load, of several hundreds, brought about the 25th, to Annapolis ; and out of the whole number only three individuals were able to walk from the boat. The rest were carried ashore and laid down in one place or another. Can those be *men*—those little livid-brown, ash-streak'd, monkey-looking dwarfs ?—are they really not mummied, dwindled corpses ? They lay there, most of them, quite still, but with a horrible look in their eyes and skinny lips, often with not enough flesh on the lips to cover their teeth. Probably no more appaling sight was ever seen on this earth. (There are deeds, crimes, that may be forgiven ; but this is not among them. It steeps its perpetrators in blackest, escapeless, endless damnation. Over 50,000 have been compell'd to die the death of starvation—reader, did you ever try to realize what *starvation* actually is ?—in those prisons—and in a land of plenty !)

An indescribable meanness, tyranny, aggravating course of insults, almost incredible—was evidently the rule of treatment through all the Southern military prisons. The dead there are not to be pitied as much as some of the living that come from there—if they can be call'd living—many them are mentally imbecile, and will never recuperate.[20]

Death of a Pennsylvania Soldier—Frank H. Irwin, Co. E, 93rd Pennsylvania—Died May 1, '65—My letter to his mother.

Dear Madam : No doubt you and Frank's friends have heard the sad fact of his death in Hospital here, through

his uncle, or the lady from Baltimore, who took his things.
(I have not seen them, only heard of them visiting Frank.)
I will write you a few lines—as a casual friend that sat by
his death bed.

Your son, Corporal Frank H. Irwin, was wounded near
Fort Fisher, Virginia, March 25th, 1865—the wound was in
the left knee, pretty bad. He was sent up to Washington,
was receiv'd in Ward C, Armory Square Hospital, March
28th—the wound became worse, and on the 4th of April
the leg was amputated a little above the knee—the operation was perform'd by Dr. Bliss, one of the best surgeons
in the army—he did the whole operation himself—there
was a good deal of bad matter gather'd—the bullet was
found in the knee. For a couple of weeks afterwards he was
doing pretty well. I visited and sat by him frequently, as he
was fond of having me. The last ten or twelve days of April
I saw that his case was critical. He previously had some
fever, with cold spells. The last week in April he was much
of the time flighty—but always mild and gentle. He died
first of May. The actual cause of death was Pyæmia, (the
absorption of the matter in the system instead of its discharge.)

Frank, as far as I saw, had everything requisite in surgical treatment, nursing, &c. He had watches much of the
time. He was so good and well-behaved, and affectionate,
I myself liked him very much. I was in the habit of coming
in afternoons and sitting by him, and soothing him, and
he liked to have me—liked to put his arm out and lay his
hand on my knee—would keep it so a long while. Toward

the last he was more restless and flighty at night—often fancied himself with his regiment—by his talk sometimes seem'd as if his feelings were hurt by being blamed by his officers for something he was entirely innocent of—said, "I never in my life was thought capable of such a thing, and never was." At other times he would fancy himself talking as it seem'd to children or such like, his relatives I suppose, and giving them good advice ; would talk to them a long while. All the time he was out of his head not one single bad word or thought or idea escaped him. It was remark'd that many a man's conversation in his senses was not half as good as Frank's delirium.

He was perfectly willing to die—he had become very weak and had suffer'd a good deal, and was perfectly resign'd, poor boy. I do not know his past life, but I feel as if it must have been good. At any rate what I saw of him here, under the most trying circumstances, with a painful wound, and among strangers, I can say that he behaved so brave, so composed, and so sweet and affectionate, it could not be surpass'd. And now like many other noble and good men, after serving his country as a soldier, he has yielded up his young life at the very outset in her service. Such things are gloomy—yet there is a text, "God doeth all things well,"—the meaning of which, after due time, appears to the soul.

I thought perhaps a few words, though from a stranger, about your son, from one who was with him at the last, might be worth while, for I loved the young man, though I but saw him immediately to lose him. I am merely a friend visiting the Hospitals occasionally to cheer the wounded and sick.

W. W.

May 7—(Sunday.)

To-day as I was walking a mile or two south of Alexandria, I fell in with several large squads of the returning Western Army, (*Sherman's men* as they call'd themselves) about a thousand in all, the largest portion of them half sick, some convalescents, &c. These fragmentary excerpts, with the unmistakable western physiognomy and idioms, crawling along slowly—after a great campaign, blown this way, as it were, out of their latitude—I mark'd with curiosity, and talk'd with off and on for over an hour. Here and there was one very sick ; but all were able to walk, except some of the last, who had given out, and were seated on the ground, faint and despondent. These I tried to cheer, told them the camp they were to reach, (a sort of half-hospital,) was only a little way further over the hill, and so got them up and started on, accompanying some of the worst a little way, and helping them, or putting them under the support of stronger comrades.

May 21.

Saw General Sheridan and his Cavalry to-day. It was a strong, attractive, serious sight. We have been having rainy weather. The men were mostly young, (a few middle-aged,) superb-looking fellows, brown, spare, keen, with well-worn clothing, many with pieces of water-proof cloth around their shoulders and hanging down. They dash'd along pretty fast, in wide close ranks, all spatter'd with mud ; no holiday soldiers. Quite all Americans (The Americans are the handsomest race that ever trod the earth.) They came clattering along, brigade after brigade. I could have watch'd for a week. Sheridan stood on a balcony, under a big tree, coolly smoking a cigar. His looks and manner impress'd me favorably.

May 22.

Have been taking a walk along Pennsylvania Avenue and Seventh street north. The city is full of soldiers, running around loose. Officers everywhere, of all grades. All have the weather-beaten look of practical service. It is a sight I never tire of. All the Armies are now here (or portions of them,) for to-morrow's Review. You see them swarming like bees everywhere.

The Grand Review.

For two days now the broad spaces of Pennsylvania Avenue along to Treasury Hill, and so by detour around to the President's House, (and so up to Georgetown, and across the Aqueduct bridge,) have been alive with a magnificent sight, the returning Armies. In their wide ranks stretching clear across the Avenue I watch them march or ride along, at a brisk pace, through two whole days—Infantry, Cavalry, Artillery— some 200,000 men......... Some days afterwards one or two other Corps.......and then, still afterwards, a good part of Sherman's immense Army, brought up from Charleston, Savannah, &c.

Western Soldiers—May 26–7.

The streets, the public buildings and grounds of Washington still swarm with soldiers from Illinois, Indiana, Ohio, Missouri, Iowa, and all the Western States. I am continually meeting and talking with them. They often speak to me first, and always show great sociability, and glad to have a good interchange of chat.......These Western soldiers are more slow in their movements, and in their intellectual quality also ; have no extreme alertness. They are larger in size, have a more serious physiognomy, are continually looking at you as they pass in the street. They are largely animal, and handsomely so. (During the War I have been at times with the Fourteenth, Fifteenth, Seventeenth, and Twentieth Corps.) I always feel drawn toward the men, and like their personal contact when we are crowded close together, as frequently these days in the street-cars. They all think the world of General Sherman ; call him "Old Bill," or sometimes "Uncle Billy."

May 28.

As I sat by the bedside of a sick Michigan soldier in a Hospital to-day, a convalescent from the adjoining bed rose and came to me, and presently we began talking. He was a middle-aged man, belonged to the 2d Virginia regiment, but lived in Racine, Ohio, and had a family there. He spoke of President Lincoln, and said : "The war is over, and many are lost. And now we have lost the best, the fairest, the truest man in America. Take him altogether he was the best man this country ever produced. It was quite a while I thought very different ; but some time before the murder, that's the way I have seen it."......There was deep earnestness in the soldier. (I found upon further talk he had known Mr. Lincoln personally, and quite closely, years before.) He was a veteran ; was now in the fifth year of his service ; was a cavalry man, and had been in a good deal of hard fighting.

Two Brothers, one South, one North—May 28-9.

I staid to-night a long time by the bed-side of a new patient, a young Baltimorean, aged about 19 years, W. S. P., (2nd Md. Southern,) very feeble, right leg amputated, can't sleep hardly at all—has taken a great deal of morphine, which, as usual, is costing more than it comes to. Evidently very intelligent and well bred—very affectionate—held on to my hand, and put it by his face, not willing to let me leave. As I was lingering, soothing him in his pain, he says to me suddenly, "I hardly think you know who I am—I don't wish to impose upon you—I am a rebel soldier." I said I did not know that, but it made no difference.......Visiting him daily for about two weeks after that, while he lived, (death had mark'd him, and he was quite alone,) I loved him much, always kiss'd him, and he did me.

In an adjoining Ward I found his brother, an officer of rank, a Union soldier, a brave and religious man, (Col. Clifton K. Prentiss, Sixth Md. Infantry, Sixth Corps, wounded in one of the engagements at Petersburgh, April 2—linger'd, suffer'd much, died in Brooklyn, Aug. 20, '65.) It was in the same battle both were hit. One was a strong Unionist, the other Secesh ; both fought on their respective sides, both badly wounded, and both brought together here after absence of four years. Each died for his cause.

May 31.

James H. Williams, age 21, 3d Va. Cavalry.—About as mark'd a case of a strong man brought low by a complication of diseases, (laryngytis, fever, debility and diarrhoea,) as I have ever seen—has superb physique, remains swarthy yet, and flush'd and red with fever—is altogether flighty—flesh of his great breast and arms tremulous, and pulse pounding away with treble quickness—lies a good deal of the time in a partial sleep, but with low muttering and groans—a sleep in which there is no rest. Powerful as he is, and so young, he will not be able to stand many more days of the strain and sapping heat of yesterday and to-day.

His throat is in a bad way, tongue and lips parch'd. When I ask him how he feels, he is able just to articulate, "I feel pretty bad yet, old man," and looks at me with his great bright eyes. Father, John Williams, Millensport, Ohio.

June 9–10.

I have been sitting late to-night by the bed-side of a wounded Captain, a friend of mine, lying with a painful fracture of left leg in one of the Hospitals, in a large Ward partially vacant. The lights were put out, all but a little candle, far from where I sat. The full moon shone in through the windows, making long, slanting silvery patches on the floor. All was still, my friend too was silent, but could not sleep ; so I sat there by him, slowly wafting the fan, and occupied with the musings that arose out of the scene, the long shadowy Ward, the beautiful ghostly moon-light on the floor, the white beds, here and there an occupant with huddled form, the bed-clothes thrown off.

The Hospitals have a number of cases of sun-stroke and exhaustion by heat, from the late Reviews. There are many such from the Sixth Corps, from the hot parade of day before yester-day. (Some of these shows cost the lives of scores of men.)

Sunday, Sep. 10.

Visited Douglas and Stanton Hospitals. They are quite full. Many of the cases are bad ones, lingering wounds, and old cases of sickness. There is a more than usual look of despair on the countenances of many of the men ; hope has left them.......I went through the Wards talking as usual. There are several here from the Confederate army, whom I had seen in other Hospitals, and they recognized me. Two were in a dying condition.

Calhoun's Real Monument.

In one of the Hospital tents for special cases, as I sat to-day tending a new amputation, I heard a couple of neighboring soldiers talking to each other from their cots. One down with fever, but improving, had come up belated from Charleston not long before. The other was what we now call an "old veteran" (*i.e.,* he was a Connecticut youth, probably of less than the age of twenty-five years, the four last of which he had spent in active service in the War in all parts of the country.) The two were chatting of one thing and another. The fever soldier spoke of John C. Calhoun's monument, which he had seen, and was describing it. The veteran said : "*I* have seen Calhoun's monument. *That* you saw is not the real monument. But I have seen it. It is the desolated, ruined South ; nearly the whole generation of young men between seventeen and fifty destroyed or maim'd ; all the old families used up—the rich impoverish'd, the plantations cover'd with weeds, the slaves unloos'd and become the masters, and the name of Southerner blacken'd with every shame—all *that* is Calhoun's *real* monument."[21]

October 3.

There are only two Army Hospitals now remaining. I went to the largest of these (Douglas) and spent the afternoon and evening. There are many sad cases, some old wounds, some of incurable sickness, and some of the wounded from the March and April battles before Richmond........(Few realize how sharp and bloody those closing battles were. Our men exposed themselves more than usual; press'd ahead, without urging. Then the Southerners fought with extra desperation. Both sides knew that with the successful chasing of the rebel cabal from Richmond, and the occupation of that city by the National troops, the game was up. The dead and wounded were unusually many.......Of the wounded, both our own and the rebel, the last lingering driblets have been brought to Hospital here. I find many rebel wounded here, and have been extra busy to-day 'tending to the worst cases of them with the rest.)

Oct., Nov. and Dec., '65 — (Sundays.)

Every Sunday of these months visited Harewood Hospital out in the woods, pleasant and recluse, some two and a half or three miles north of the Capitol. The situation is healthy, with broken ground, grassy slopes and patches of oak woods, the trees large and fine. It was one of the most extensive of the Hospitals — but now reduced to four or five partially occupied Wards, the numerous others being entirely vacant. The patients are the leavings of the other Hospitals ; many of them very sad cases indeed. In November, this became the last Military Hospital kept up by the Government, all the others being closed. Cases of the worst and most incurable wounds, and obstinate illness, and of poor fellows who have no homes to go to, are found here.

Dec. 10 — (Sunday.)

Again spending a good part of the day at Harewood. As I write this, it is about an hour before sundown. I have walk'd out for a few minutes to the edge of the woods to soothe myself with the hour and scene. It is a glorious, warm, golden-sunny, still afternoon. The only noise here is from a crowd of cawing crows, on some trees three hundred yards distant. Clusters of gnats swimming and dancing in the air in all directions. The oak leaves are thick under the bare trees, and give a strong and delicious perfume.......Inside the Wards every thing is gloomy. Death is there. As I enter'd, I was confronted by it, the first thing. A corpse of a poor soldier, just dead, of typhoid fever. The attendants had just straighten'd the limbs, put coppers on the eyes, and were laying it out.

Three Years Summ'd Up.

During my past three years in Hospital, camp or field, I made over 600 visits or tours, and went, as I estimate, among from 80,000 to

100,000 of the wounded and sick, as sustainer of spirit and body in some degree, in time of need. These visits varied from an hour or two, to all day or night ; for with dear or critical cases I always watch'd all night. Sometimes I took up my quarters in the Hospital, and slept or watch'd there several nights in succession. Those three years I consider the greatest privilege and satisfaction, (with all their feverish excitements and physical deprivations and lamentable sights,) and, of course, the most profound lesson and reminiscence, of my life. I can say that in my ministerings I comprehended all, whoever came in my way, Northern or Southern, and slighted none. It afforded me, too, the perusal of those subtlest, rarest, divinest volumes of Humanity, laid bare in its inmost recesses, and of actual life and death, better than the finest, most labor'd narratives, histories, poems in the libraries. It arous'd and brought out and decided undream'd-of depths of emotion. It has given me my plainest and most fervent views of the true *ensemble* and extent of The States. While I was with wounded and sick in thousands of cases from the New England States, and from New York, New Jersey, and Pennsylvania, and from Michigan, Wisconsin, Ohio, Indiana, Illinois, and all the Western States, I was with more or less from all the States, North and South, without exception. I was with many from the Border States, especially from Maryland and Virginia, and found, during those lurid years 1862 — 65, far more Union Southerners, especially Tennesseans, than is supposed. I was with many rebel officers and men among our wounded, and gave them always what I had, and tried to cheer them the same as any. I was among the army teamsters considerably, and, indeed, always found myself drawn to them. Among the black soldiers, wounded or sick, and in the contraband camps, I also took my way whenever in their neighborhood, and did what I could for them.

The Million Dead, too, summ'd up—The Unknown.

The Dead in this War—there they lie, strewing the fields and woods and valleys and battle-fields of the South—Virginia, the Peninsula—Malvern Hill and Fair Oaks—the banks of the Chickahominy—the terraces of Fredericksburgh—Antietam bridge—the grisly ravines of Manassas—the bloody promenade of the Wilderness—the varieties of the *strayed* dead, (the estimate of the War Department is 25,000 National soldiers kill'd in battle and never buried at all, 5,000 drown'd—15,000 inhumed strangers or on the march in haste, in hitherto unfound localities—2,000 graves cover'd by sand and mud, by Mississippi freshets, 3,000 carried away by caving-in of banks, &c.,)—Gettysburgh, the West, Southwest—Vicksburg—Chattanooga—the trenches of Petersburgh—the numberless battles, camps, Hospitals everywhere—the crop reap'd by the mighty reapers, Typhoid, Dysentery, Inflammations—and blackest and loathesomest of all, the dead and living burial-pits, the Prison-Pens of Andersonville, Salisbury, Belle-Isle, &c., (not Dante's pictured Hell and all its woes, its degradations, filthy torments, excell'd those Prisons)—the dead, the dead, the dead—*our* dead, or South or North, ours all, (all, all, all, finally dear to me)—or East or West—Atlantic Coast or Mississippi Valley—Some where they crawl'd to die, alone, in bushes, low gulleys, or on the sides of hills—(there, in secluded spots, their skeletons, bleach'd bones, tufts of hair, buttons, fragments of clothing, are occasionally found, yet)—our young men once so handsome and so joyous, taken from us—the son from the mother, the husband from the wife, the dear friend from the dear friend—the clusters of camp graves, in Georgia, the Carolinas, and in Tennessee—the single graves in the woods or by the road-side, (hundreds, thousands, obliterated)—the corpses floated down the rivers, and caught and lodged, (dozens, scores, floated down the Upper Potomac, after the cavalry engagements, the pursuit of Lee, following Gettysburgh)—some lie at the bottom of the sea—the general Million, and the special Cemeteries in almost all the States—the Infinite Dead—(the land entire is saturated, perfumed with their impalpable ashes' exhalation in Nature's chemistry distill'd, and shall be so forever, and every grain of wheat and ear of corn, and every flower that grows, and every breath we draw,)—not only Northern dead leavening Southern soil—thousands, aye many tens of thousands, Southerners, crumble to-day in Northern earth.

And everywhere among these countless graves—everywhere in the many Soldiers Cemeteries of the Nation, (there are over seventy of them)—as at the time in the vast trenches, the depositaries of slain, Northern and Southern, after the great battles—not only where the scathing trail pass'd those years, but radiating since in all the peaceful quarters of the land—we see, and see, and ages yet may see, on monuments and gravestones, singly or in masses, to thousands or tens of thousands, the significant word

UNKNOWN.

(In some of the Cemeteries nearly *all* the dead are Unknown. At Salisbury, N. C., for instance, the known are only 85, while the Unknown are 12,027, and 11,700 of these are buried in trenches. A National Monument has been put up here, by order of Congress, to mark the spot—but what visible, material monument can ever fittingly commemorate the spot ?)

As I write this conclusion—in the open air, latter part of June, 1875, a delicious forenoon, everything rich and fresh from last night's copious rain—ten years and more have pass'd away since that War, and its wholesale deaths, burials, graves. (*They* make indeed the true Memoranda of the War—mute, subtle, immortal.) From ten years' rain and snow, in their seasons—grass, clover, pine trees, orchards, forests—from all the noiseless miracles of soil and sun and running streams—how peaceful and how beautiful appear to-day even the Battle-Trenches, and the many hundred thousand Cemetery mounds ! Even at Andersonville, to-day, innocence and a smile. (A late account says, 'The stockade has fallen to decay, is grown upon, and a season more will efface it entirely, except from our hearts and memories. The *dead line,* over which so many brave soldiers pass'd to the freedom of eternity rather than endure the misery of life, can only be traced here and there, for most of the old marks the last ten years have obliterated. The thirty-five wells, which the prisoners dug with cups and spoons, remain just as they were left. And the wonderful spring which was discover'd one morning, after a thunder storm, flowing down the hillside, still yields its sweet, pure water as freely now as then. The Cemetery, with its thirteen thousand graves, is on the slope of a beautiful hill. Over the quiet spot already trees give the cool shade which would have been so gratefully sought by the poor fellows whose lives were ended under the scorching sun.')

And now, to thought of these—on these graves of the dead of the War, as on an altar—to memory of these, or North or South, I close and dedicate my book.

NOTES.

'Convulsiveness.'

As I have look'd over the proof-sheets of the preceding Memoranda, I have once or twice fear'd that my little tract would prove, at best, but a batch of convulsively written reminiscences. Well, be it so. They are but items, parts of the actual distraction, heat, smoke and excitement of those times—of the qualities that then and there took shape. The War itself with the temper of society preceding it, can indeed be best described by that very word, *Convulsiveness.*

Typical Soldiers.

Even the typical soldiers I was personally intimate with, and knew well—it seems to me if I were to make a list of them it would be like a City Directory. Some few only have I mention'd in the foregoing pages—most are dead—a few yet living. There is Reuben Farwell, of Michigan, (little 'Mitch ;') Benton H. Wilson, color-bearer, 185th New York ; Wm. Stansberry ; Manvill Winterstein, Ohio ; Bethuel Smith ; Capt. Simms, of 51st New

York, (kill'd at Petersburg mine explosion,) Capt. Sam. Pooley and Lieut. Fred. McReady, same Reg't. Also, same Reg't., my brother, Geo. W. Whitman—in '61 a young man working in Brooklyn as a carpenter—was not supposed to have any taste for soldiering—but volunteer'd in the ranks at once on the breaking out of the War—continued in active service all through, four years, re-enlisting twice—was promoted, step by step, (several times immediately after battles,) Lieutenant, Captain, Major and Lieut. Colonel—was in the actions at Roanoke, Newbern, 2d Bull Run, Chantilly, South Mountain, Antietam, Fredericks-burgh, Vicksburgh, Jackson, the bloody conflicts of the Wilder-ness, and at Spottsylvania [sic], Cold Harbor, and afterwards around Petersburg. At one of these latter he was taken prisoner, and pass'd four or five months in Secesh military prisons, nar-rowly escaping with life, from a severe fever, from starvation and half-nakedness in the winter.

[What a history that 51st New York had ! Went out early—march'd, fought everywhere—was in storms at sea, nearly wreck'd—storm'd forts—tramp'd hither and yon in Virginia, night and day, summer of '62—afterwards Kentucky and Missis-sippi—re-enlisted—was in all the engagements and campaigns, as above.]

I strengthen and comfort myself much with the certainty that the capacity for just such Regiments, (hundreds, thousands of them) is inexhaustible in the United States, and that there isn't a County nor a Township in The Republic—nor a street in any City—but could turn out, and, on occasion, *would* turn out, lots of just such *Typical Soldiers,* whenever wanted.

Before I went down to the Field, and among the Hospitals, I

had my hours of doubt about These States ; but not since. The
bulk of the Army, to me, develop'd, transcended, in personal
qualities—and, radically, in moral ones—all that the most enthu-
siastic Democratic-Republican ever fancied, idealized in loftiest
dreams. And curious as it may seem, the War, to me, *proved*
Humanity, and proved America and the Modern.

(I think I am perfectly well aware of the corruption and
wickedness of my lands and days—the general political, business
and social shams and shysterisms, everywhere. Heaven knows, I
see enough of them—running foul of them continually ! But I
also see the noblest elements in society—and not in specimens
only, but vast, enduring, inexhaustible strata of them—rugged-
ness, simplicity, courage, love, wit, health, liberty, patriotism—
all the virtues, the main bulk, public and private.)

Attack on Fort Sumter, April, 1861.

What ran through the Land, as if by electric nerves, and show'd
itself in stupendous and practical action, immediately after the
firing on *the Flag* at Fort Sumter—the Nation ('till then incredulous) flush'd in the face, and all its veins fiercely pulsing and
pounding—the arm'd volunteers instantaneously springing up
everywhere—the tumultuous processions of the regiments—
Was it not grand to have lived in such scenes and days, and be
absorb'd by them, and unloosen'd to them ?

The news of the attack on Sumter was receiv'd in New York
city late at night, (13th April, 1861,) and was immediately sent
out in extras of the newspapers. I had been to the opera in Four-

teenth street that night, and after the performance, was walking down Broadway toward twelve o'clock, on my way to Brooklyn, when I heard in the distance the loud cries of the newsboys, who came presently tearing and yelling up the street, rushing from side to side even more furiously than usual. I bought an extra and cross'd to the Metropolitan Hotel (Niblo's,) where the great lamps were still brightly blazing, and, with a small crowd of others, who gather'd impromptu, read the news, which was evidently authentic. For the benefit of some who had no papers, one of us read the telegram aloud, while all listen'd silently and attentively. No remark was made by any of the crowd, which had increas'd to thirty or forty, but all stood a minute or two, I remember, before they dispers'd. I can almost see them there now, under the lamps at midnight again.

The ensuing three Months—The National Uprising and Volunteering.

I have said in another place that the three Presidentiads preceding 1861 show'd how the weakness and wickedness of rulers are just as eligible here in America under republican, as in Europe under dynastic influences.[22] But what can I say of that prompt and splendid wrestling with Secession-Slavery, the arch enemy personified, the instant he unmistakably show'd his face ? ......The volcanic upheaval of the Nation, after that firing on the flag at Charleston, proved for certain something which had been previously in great doubt, and at once substantially settled the question of Disunion. In my judgment it will remain as the

grandest and most encouraging spectacle yet vouchsafed in any
age, old or new, to political progress and Democracy. It was not
for what came to the surface merely—though that was important ; but what it indicated below, which was of eternal importance.......Down in the abysms of New World humanity there
had form'd and harden'd a primal hardpan of National Union
Will, determin'd and in the majority, refusing to be tamper'd
with or argued against, confronting all emergencies, and capable
at any time of bursting all surface-bonds, and breaking out like
an earthquake. It is indeed the best lesson of the century, or of
America, and it is a mighty privilege to have been part of
it.......(Two great spectacles, immortal proofs of Democracy,
unequall'd in all the history of the past, are furnish'd by this
War—one at the beginning, the other at its close. Those are—
the general Voluntary Armed Upheaval—and the peaceful and
harmonious Disbanding of the Armies, in the summer of 1865.)

Contemptuous National feeling.

Even after the bombardment of Sumter, however, the gravity of
the revolt, and the power and will of the Slave States for a strong
and continued military resistance to National authority, was not
at all realized through the North, except by a few. Nine-tenths of
the people of the Free States look'd upon the rebellion, as started
in South Carolina, from a feeling one-half of contempt and the
other half composed of anger and incredulity. It was not
thought it would be join'd in by Virginia, North Carolina or
Georgia. A great and cautious National official predicted that it

would blow over 'in sixty days,' and folks generally believ'd the prediction. I remember talking about it on a Fulton ferry-boat with the Brooklyn Mayor, who said he only 'hoped the Southern fire-eaters would commit some overt act of resistance, as they would then be at once so effectually squelch'd, we would never hear of Secession again—but he was afraid they never would have the pluck to really do anything.'.......I remember too that a couple of companies of the Thirteenth Brooklyn, who ren-dezvou'd at the City Armory, and started thence as Thirty Days' Men, were all provided with pieces of rope conspicuously tied to their musket barrels, with which to bring back each man a pris-oner from the audacious South, to be led in a noose, on our men's early and triumphal return ! [This was indeed the general feeling, and came to the surface. Still, there was a very strong Secession party at the North, as I shall mention in a Note further on.]

Battle of Bull Run, July, 1861.

All this sort of feeling was destin'd to be arrested and cut short and revers'd by a terrible shock—the battle of First Bull Run— certainly, as we now know it, one of the most singular fights on record. (All battles, and their results, are far more matters of accident than is generally thought ; but this was throughout a casualty, a chance. Each side supposed it had won, till the last moment. One had in point of fact just the same right to be routed as the other. By a fiction, or series of fictions, the

National forces, at the last moment, exploded in a panic, and fled from the field.)

The troops commenced pouring into Washington, over the Long Bridge, at day-light on Monday 22d—day drizzling all through with rain.

The Saturday and Sunday of the battle, (20th, 21st,) had been parch'd and hot to an extreme—the dust, the grime and smoke, in layers, sweated in, follow'd by other layers, again sweated in, absorb'd by those excited souls—their clothes all saturated with the clay-powder filling the air—stirr'd up everywhere on the dry-roads and trodden fields, by the regiments, swarming wagons, artillery, &c.—all the men, with this coating of murk and sweat and Virginia rain—now recoiling back—pouring over the Long Bridge, a horrible march of twenty miles, returning to Washington baffled, humiliated, panic-struck !......Where are the vaunts, and the proud boasts with which you went forth ? Where are your banners, and your bands of music, and your ropes to bring back your prisoners ? Well, there isn't a band playing—and there isn't a flag but clings ashamed and lank to its staff......The sun rises, but shines not. The men appear, at first sparsely and shame-faced enough—then thicker in the streets of Washington —appear in Pennsylvania avenue, and on the steps and basement entrances. They come along in disorderly mobs, some in squads, stragglers, companies. Occasionally, a rare regiment, in perfect order, with its officers (some gaps, dead, the true braves,) marching in silence, with lowering faces, stern, weary to sinking, all black and dirty, but every man with his musket, and stepping alive ;—but these are the exceptions.......Sidewalks of Pennsylvania avenue, Fourteenth street, &c., crowded, jamm'd with citizens, darkies, clerks, everybody, lookers-on ; women in the windows, curious expressions from faces, as those swarms of dirt-cover'd return'd soldiers there (will they never end ?) move by ; but nothing said, no comments ; (half our lookers-on Secesh of the most venomous kind—they say nothing ; but the devil snickers in their faces.)

During the forenoon Washington gets motley with the dirt-cover'd soldiers—queer-looking objects, strange eyes and faces, drench'd (the steady rain drizzles on all day) and fearfully worn, hungry, haggard, blister'd in the feet. Good people (but not over-many of them either,) hurry up something for their grub. They put wash-kettles on the fire, for soup, for coffee. They set tables on the side-walks—wagon loads of bread are purchas'd, swiftly cut in stout chunks. Here are two aged ladies, beautiful, the first in the city for culture and charm, they stand with store of eating and drink at an improvised table of rough plank, and give food, and have the store replenish'd from their house every half-hour all that day ; and there in the rain they stand, active, silent, white-hair'd, and give food, though the tears stream down their cheeks, almost without intermission, the whole time.

Amid the deep excitement, crowds and motion, and desperate eagerness, it seems strange to see many, very many, of the soldiers sleeping—in the midst of all, sleeping sound. They drop down anywhere, on the steps of houses, up close by the basements or fences, on the sidewalk, aside on some vacant lot, and deeply sleep. A poor seventeen or eighteen year old boy lies

there, on the stoop of a grand house ; he sleeps so calmly, so profoundly ! Some clutch their muskets firmly even in sleep. Some
in squads ; comrades, brothers, close together—and on them, as
they lay, sulkily drips the rain.

As afternoon pass'd, and evening came, the streets, the bar-
rooms, knots everywhere, listeners, questioners, terrible yarns,
bugaboo, mask'd batteries, our regiment all cut up, &c.,—
stories and story-tellers, windy, bragging, vain centres of street-
crowds. Resolution, manliness, seem to have abandon'd Washington. The principal hotel, Willard's, is full of shoulder-
straps—thick, crush'd, creeping with shoulder-straps. (I see
them, and must have a word with them. There you are, shoulder-straps !—but where are your companies ? where are your
men ? Incompetents ! never tell me of chances of battle, of getting stray'd, and the like. I think this is your work, this retreat,
after all. Sneak, blow, put on airs there in Willard's sumptuous
parlors and bar-rooms, or anywhere—no explanation shall save
you. Bull Run is your work ; had you been half or one-tenth
worthy your men, this would never have happen'd.)

Meantime, in Washington, among the great persons and their
entourage, a mixture of awful consternation, uncertainty, rage,
shame, helplessness, and stupefying disappointment ! The worst
not only imminent, but already here. In a few hours—perhaps
before the next meal—the Secesh generals, with their victorious
hordes, will be upon us. The dream of Humanity, the vaunted
Union we thought so strong, so impregnable—lo ! it is smash'd
like a china plate. One bitter, bitter hour—perhaps proud America will never again know such a bitter hour. She must pack and

fly—no time to spare. Those white palaces—the dome-crown'd Capitol there on the hill, so stately over the trees—shall they be left—or destroy'd first ?.......For it is certain that the talk among the magnates and officers and clerks and officials everywhere, for twenty-four hours in and around Washington, after Bull Run, was loud and undisguised for yielding out and out, and substituting the Southern rule, and Lincoln promptly abdicating and departing. If the Secesh officers and forces had immediately follow'd, and by a bold Napoleonic movement, had enter'd Washington the first day, (or even the second,) they could have had things their own way, and a powerful faction North to back them. One of our returning officers express'd in public that night, amid a swarm of officers and gentlemen in a crowded room, the opinion that it was useless to fight, that the Southerners had made their title clear to their own terms, and that the best course for the National Government to pursue was to desist from any further attempt at stopping them, and admit them again to the lead on the best terms they were willing to grant. Not a voice was rais'd against this judgment amid that large crowd of officers and gentlemen. (The fact is, the hour was one of the three or four of those crises we had during the fluctuations of four years, when human eyes appear'd at least just as likely to see the last breath of the Union as to see it continue.)

But the hour, the day, the night pass'd, and whatever returns, an hour, a day, a night like that can never again return. The President, recovering himself, begins that very night—sternly, rapidly sets about the work of reorganizing his forces, and placing himself in positions for future and greater work. If there were nothing else of Abraham Lincoln for history to stamp him with, it is enough to send him with his wreath to the memory of all future time, that he endured that hour, that day, bitterer than gall—indeed a crucifixion day—that it did not conquer him— that he unflinchingly stemm'd it, and resolv'd to lift himself and the Union out of it.

Then the great New York papers at once appear'd, (commencing that very evening, and following it up the next morning, and incessantly through many days afterwards,) with leaders that rang out over the land, with the loudest, most reverberating ring of clearest, wildest bugles, full of encouragement, hope, inspiration, unfaltering defiance. Those magnificent editorials ! they never flagg'd for a fortnight. The *Herald* commenced them—I remember the articles well. The *Tribune* was equally cogent and inspiriting—and the *Times, Evening Post,* and other principal papers, were not a whit behind. They came in good time, for they were needed. For in the humiliation of Bull Run, the popular feeling North, from its extreme of superciliousness, recoil'd to the depth of gloom and apprehension.

(Of all the days of the War, there are two especially I can never forget. Those were the day following the news, in New York and Brooklyn, of that first Bull Run defeat, and the day of Abraham Lincoln's death. I was home in Brooklyn on both occasions. The day of the murder we heard the news very early in the morning. Mother prepared breakfast—and other meals afterward—as usual ; but not a mouthful was eaten all day by either of us. We each drank half a cup of coffee ; that was all. Little was said. We got every newspaper morning and evening, and the frequent extras of that period, and pass'd them silently to each other.)

Sherman's Army's Jubilation, 1865 — Its sudden stoppage.

When Sherman's Armies, (long after they left Atlanta,) were marching through South and North Carolina—after leaving Savannah, the news of Lee's capitulation having been receiv'd— the men never mov'd a mile without from some part of the line sending up continued, inspiriting shouts and cries. At intervals every little while, all day long, sounded out the wild music of those peculiar army cries. They would be commenc'd by one regiment or brigade, immediately taken up by others, and at length whole corps and Armies would join in these wild triumphant choruses. It was one of the characteristic expressions of the western troops, and became a habit, serving as relief and outlet to the men—a vent for their feelings of victory, returning peace, &c. Morning, noon, and afternoon, spontaneous, for occasion, or without occasion, these huge, strange cries, differing from any other, echoing though the open air for many a mile, expressing youth, joy, wildness, irrepressible strength, and the ideas of advance and conquest, sounded along the swamps and uplands of the South, floating to the skies. ('There never were men that kept in better spirits, in danger or defeat—what then could they do in victory ?'—said one of the 15th. Corps to me, afterwards.)

This exuberance continued till the Armies arrived at Raleigh. There the news of the President's murder was receiv'd. Then no more shouts or yells, for a week. All the marching was comparatively muffled. It was very significant—hardly a loud word or laugh in many of the regiments. A hush and silence pervaded all.

Attitude of Foreign Governments
toward the U.S. during the War of 1861–'65.

Looking over my scraps, I find I wrote the following during 1864, or the latter part of '63 :

The happening to our America, abroad as well as at home, these years, is indeed most strange. The Democratic Republic has paid her to-day the terrible and resplendent compliment of the united wish of all the nations of the world that her Union should be broken, her future cut off, and that she should be compell'd to descend to the level of kingdoms and empires ordinarily great ! There is certainly not one government in Europe but is now watching the war in this country, with the ardent prayer that the United States may be effectually split, crippled, and dismember'd by it. There is not one but would help toward that dismemberment, if it dared. I say such is the ardent wish to-day of England and of France, as governments, and of all the nations of Europe, as governments. I think indeed it is to-day the real, heartfelt wish of all the nations of the world, with the single exception of Mexico—Mexico, the only one to whom we have ever really done wrong, and now the only one who prays for us and for our triumph, with genuine prayer.

Is it not indeed strange ? America, made up of all, cheerfully

from the beginning opening her arms to all, the result and jus-
tifier of all, of Britain, Germany, France and Spain—all here—
the accepter, the friend, hope, last resource and general house
of all—she who has harm'd none, but been bounteous to so
many, to millions, the mother of strangers and exiles, all
nations—should now I say be paid this dread compliment of
general governmental fear and hatred ?.......Are we indignant ?
alarm'd ? Do we feel wrong'd ? jeopardized ? No ; help'd,
braced, concentrated, rather. We are all too prone to wander
from ourselves, to affect Europe, and watch her frowns and
smiles. We need this hot lesson of general hatred, and henceforth must never forget it. Never again will we trust the moral
sense nor abstract friendliness of a single *government* of the old
world.

No good Portrait of Abraham Lincoln.

Probably the reader has seen physiognomies (often old farmers, sea-captains, and such) that, behind their homeliness, or
even ugliness, held superior points so subtle, yet so palpable,
defying the lines of art, making the real life of their faces almost
as impossible to depict as a wild perfume or fruit-taste, or a
passionate tone of the living voice..... and such was Lincoln's
face, the peculiar color, the lines of it, the eyes, mouth, expression, &c. Of technical *beauty* it had nothing—but to the eye of
a great artist it furnished a rare study, a feast and fascination.......The current portraits are all failures—most of them
caricatures.

The War, though with two sides, really ONE IDENTITY
(as struggles, furious conflicts of Nature, for final harmony.)
*—The Soil it bred and ripen'd from—the North as responsible
for it as the South.*

Of the War of Attempted Secession—the greatest National event
of the first Century of the United States, and one among the
great events of all Centuries—the main points of its origin, and
the *conditions* out of which it arose, are full of lessons, full of
warnings yet to the Republic, and always will be. The underlying and principal of those points are yet singularly ignored. The
Northern States were really just as responsible for that War, (in
its precedents, foundations, instigations,) as the South. Let me
try to give my view.

From the age of 21 to 40, (1840–'60,) I was interested in the
political movements of the land, not so much as a participant,
but as an observer, though a regular voter at the elections. I
think I was conversant with the springs of action, and their
workings, not only in New York city and Brooklyn, but understood them in the whole country, as I had made leisurely tours
through all the Middle States, and partially through the Western
and Southern, and down to New Orleans, in which city I
resided for some time. (I was there at the conclusion of the Mex-
ican War—saw and talk'd with Gen. Taylor, and the other generals and officers, who were feted and detain'd several days, on
their return victorious from that expedition.)

Of course many and very contradictory things, specialties,

prejudices, Constitutional views, &c., went to make up the origin of the War—but perhaps the most significant general fact can be best indicated and stated as follows : For twenty-five years previous to the outbreak, the controling 'Democratic' nominating conventions—starting from their primaries in wards or districts, and so expanding to counties, powerful cities, States, and to the great President-Naming Conventions—were getting to represent, and to be composed of, more and more putrid and dangerous materials. Let me give a schedule, or list, of one of these representative Conventions for a long time before, and inclusive of, that which nominated Buchanan. (Remember they had come to be the fountains and tissues of the American body politic, forming, as it were, the whole blood, legislation, office-holding, &c.) One of these Conventions from 1840 to '60 exhibited a spectacle such as could never be seen except in our own age and in These States. The members who composed it were, seven-eighths of them, office-holders, office-seekers, pimps, malignants, conspirators, murderers, fancy-men, custom-house clerks, contractors, kept-editors, spaniels well-train'd to carry and fetch, jobbers, infidels, disunionists, terrorists, mail-riflers, slave-catchers, pushers of slavery, creatures of the President, creatures of would-be Presidents, spies, blowers, electioneerers, bawlers, bribers, compromisers, lobbyers, sponges, ruined sports, expell'd gamblers, policy-backers, monte-dealers, duelists, carriers of conceal'd weapons, deaf men, pimpled men, scarr'd inside with vile disease, gaudy outside with gold chains made from the people's money and harlot's money twisted together ; crawling, serpentine men, the lousy combings and born freedom-sellers of the earth. And whence came they ? From

back-yards and bar-rooms ; from out of the custom-houses, mar-
shals' offices, post-offices, and gambling hells ; from the President's house, the jail, the station-house ; from unnamed
by-places where devilish disunion was hatched at midnight ;
from political hearses, and from the coffins inside, and from the
shrouds inside of the coffins ; from the tumors and abscesses of
the land ; from the skeletons and skulls in the vaults of the federal almshouses ; and from the running sores of the great
cities.......Such, I say, form'd the entire personnel, the atmosphere, nutriment and chyle, of our municipal, State and
National Politics—substantially permeating, handling, deciding
and wielding everything—legislation, nominations, elections,
'public sentiment' &c.,—while the great masses of the people,
farmers, mechanics and traders, were helpless in their gripe.
These conditions were mostly prevalent in the North and West,
and especially in New York and Philadelphia cities ; and the
Southern leaders, (bad enough, but of a far higher order,) struck
hands and affiliated with, and used them.......Is it strange that a
thunder-storm follow'd such morbid and stifling strata ?23

I say then, that what, as just outlined, heralded and made the
ground ready for Secession revolt, ought to be held up, through
all the future, as the most instructive lesson in American Political
History—the most significant warning and beacon-light to
coming generations......I say that the sixteenth, seventeenth and
eighteenth terms of the American Presidency have shown that
the villainy and shallowness of rulers (back'd by the machinery
of great parties) are just as eligible to These States as to any foreign despotism, kingdom, or empire—there is not a bit of difference. History is to record those three Presidentiads, and

especially the administrations of Fillmore and Buchanan, as so
far our topmost warning and shame. Never were publicly display'd more deform'd, mediocre, snivelling, unreliable, false-
hearted men ! Never were These States so insulted, and
attempted to be betray'd ! All the main purposes for which the
government was establish'd, were openly denied. The perfect
equality of slavery with freedom was flauntingly preach'd in the
North—nay, the superiority of slavery. The slave trade was pro-
posed to be renew'd. Everywhere frowns and misunderstand-
ings—everywhere exasperations and humiliations.......(The
Slavery contest is settled—and the War is over—yet do not those
putrid conditions, too many of them, still exist ? still result in
diseases, fevers, wounds—not of War and Army Hospitals—but
the wounds and diseases of Peace ?)

Out of those generic influences, mainly in New York, Pennsylvania, Ohio, &c., arose the attempt at disunion. To philosophical examination, the malignant fever of this war shows its
embryonic sources, and the original nourishment of its life and
growth, in the North. I say Secession, below the surface, originated and was brought to maturity in the Free States. I allude to
the score of years preceding 1860. The events of '61 amazed
everybody North and South, and burst all prophecies and calculations like bubbles. But even then, and during the whole War,
the stern fact remains that (not only did the North put it down,
but) *the Secession cause had numerically just as many sympathizers
in the Free as in the Rebel States.*

As to slavery, abstractly and practically, (its idea, and the
determination to establish and expand it, especially in the new

Territories, the future America,) it is too common, I say, to identify it exclusively with the South. In fact down to the opening of
the War, the whole country had about an equal hand in it. The
North had at least been just as guilty, if not more guilty ; and the
East and West had. The former Presidents and Congresses had
been guilty—the Governors and Legislatures of every Northern
State had been guilty, and the Mayors of New York and other
northern cities had all been guilty—their hands were all stain'd.

So much for that point, and for the North......As to the inception and direct instigation of the War, in the South itself, I shall
not attempt interiors or complications. Behind all, the idea that
it was from a resolute and arrogant determination on the part of
the extreme Slaveholders, the Calhounites, to carry the States
Rights' portion of the Constitutional Compact to its farthest
verge, and Nationalize Slavery, or else disrupt the Union, and
found a new Empire, with Slavery for its corner-stone, was and
is undoubtedly the true theory. (If successful, this attempt
would of course have destroy'd not only our American Republic, in anything like first-class proportions, in itself and its prestige, but for ages at least, the cause of Liberty and Equality
everywhere, and would have been the greatest triumph of reac-
tion, and the severest blow to political and every other freedom,
possible to conceive. Its worst results would have inured to the
Southern States themselves.)

That our National-Democratic experiment, principle, and
machinery, could triumphantly sustain such a shock, and that
the Constitution could weather it, like a ship a storm, and come
out of it as sound and whole as before, is by far the most signal

proof yet of the stability of that experiment, Democracy, and of those principles, and that Constitution. But the case is not fully stated at that. It is certain to me that the United States, by virtue of the Secession War and its results, and through that and them only, are now ready to enter, and must certainly enter, upon their genuine career in history, as no more torn and divided in their spinal requisites, but a great Homogeneous Nation,—Free States all—a moral and political unity in variety, such as Nature shows in her grandest physical works, and as much greater than any mere work of Nature, as the moral and political, the work of man, his mind, his soul, are, in their loftiest sense, greater than the merely physical......Out of that War not only has the Nationality of The States escaped from being strangled, but more than any of the rest, and, in my opinion, more than the North itself, the vital heart and breath of the South have escaped as from the pressure of a general nightmare, and are now to enter on a life, development, and active freedom, whose realities are certain in the future, notwithstanding all the Southern vexations and humiliations of the hour—a development which could not possibly have been achiev'd on any less terms, or by any other means than that War, or something equivalent to it. And I predict that the South is yet to outstrip the North.

Then another fact, never hitherto broach'd, Nationally— probably several facts, perhaps paradoxical—needing rectification—(for the whole sense and justice of the War must not be supposed to be confined to the Northern point of view.) Is there not some side from which the Secession cause itself has its justification ? Was there ever a great popular movement, or revolt, revolution, or attempt at revolution, without some solid basis interwoven with it, and supporting it ? at least something that could be said in behalf of it ?......We are apt to confine our view to the few more glaring and more atrocious Southern features— the arrogance of most of the leading men and politicians—the fearful crime of Slavery itself—But the time will come—perhaps has come—to begin to take a Philosophical view of the whole affair.

Already, as I write this concluding Note to my Memoranda, (Summer, 1875,) a new, maturing generation has swept in, obliterating with oceanic currents the worst reminiscences of the War ; and the passage of time has heal'd over at least its deepest scars. Already, the events of 1861–65, and the seasons that immediately preceded, as well as those that closely follow'd them, have lost their direct personal impression, and the living heat and excitement of their own time, and are being marshall'd for casting, or getting ready to be cast, into the cold and bloodless electrotype plates of History. Or, if we admit that the savage temper and wide differences of opinion, and feelings of wrongs, and mutual recriminations, that led to the War, and flamed in its mortal conflagration, may not have yet entirely burnt themselves out, the embers of them are dying embers, and a few more winters and summers, a few more rains and snows, will surely quench their fires, and leave them only as a far off memory. Already the War of Attempted Secession has become a thing of the past.

And now I have myself, in my thought, deliberately come to unite the whole conflict, both sides, the South and North, really into One, and to view it as a struggle going on within One Identity. Like any of Nature's great convulsions, wars going on within herself—not from separated sets of laws and influences, but the same—really, efforts, conflicts, most violent ones, for deeper harmony, freer and larger scope, completer homogeneousness and power.

What is any Nation, after all—and what is a human being—but a struggle between conflicting, paradoxical, opposing elements—and they themselves and their most violent contests, important parts of that One Identity, and of its development ?

Results South—Now and Hence.

The present condition of things (1875) in South Carolina, Mississippi, Louisiana, and other parts of the former Slave States—the utter change and overthrow of their whole social, and the greatest coloring feature of their political institutions—a horror and dismay, as of limitless sea and fire, sweeping over them, and substituting the confusion, chaos, and measureless degradation and insult of the present—the black domination, but little above the beasts—viewed as a temporary, deserv'd punishment for their Slavery and Secession sins, may perhaps be admissible ; but as a permanency of course is not to be consider'd for a moment. (Did the vast mass of the blacks, in Slavery in the United States, present a terrible and deeply complicated problem through the just ending century ? But how if the mass of the blacks in freedom in the U.S. all through the ensuing century, should present a yet more terrible and more deeply complicated problem ?)

The conquest of England eight centuries ago, by the Franco-

Normans—the obliteration of the old, (in many respects so needing obliteration)—the Domesday Book, and the repartition of the land—the old impedimenta removed, even by blood and ruthless violence, and a new, progressive genesis establish'd, new seeds sown—Time has proved plain enough that, bitter as they were, all these were the most salutary series of revolutions that could possibly have happen'd. Out of them, and by them mainly, have come, out of Albic, Roman and Saxon England—and without them could not have come—not only the England of the 500 years down to the present, and of the present—but These States. Nor, except for that terrible dislocation and overturn, would These States, as they are, exist to-day.

Extricating one's-self from the temporary gaucheries of the hour, can there be anything more certain than the rehabilitated prosperity of the Southern States, all and several, if their growing generations, refusing to be dismay'd by present embarrassments and darkness, accept their position in the Union as an immutable fact, and like the Middle and Western States, "fly the flag of practical industry and business, and adopting the great ideas of America with faith and courage, developing their resources, providing for education, abandoning old fictions, leave the Secession war and its bygones behind, and resolutely draw a curtain over the past" ?

I want to see the Southern States, in a better sense than ever, and under the new dispensation, again take a leading part in what is emphatically *their* Nationality as much as anybody's. Soon, soon, it will begin to be realized that out of the War, after all, *they* have gained a more substantial victory than anybody.[24]

Future History of the United States,
growing out of the War—(My Speculations.)

Our Nation's ending Century, thus far—even with the great
struggle of 1861–'65—I do not so much call the History of the
United States. Rather, our preparation, or preface. As the chief
and permanent result of those four years, and the signal triumph
of Nationalism at the end of them, now commence that History
of the United States, which, grandly developing, exfoliating,
stretching through the future, is yet to be enacted, and is only to
be really written hundreds of years hence.

And of the events of that Future—as well as the Present and
the Past, or war or peace—have they been, and will they continue to be, (does any one suppose ?) a series of *accidents,*
depending on either good luck or bad luck, as may chance to
turn out ? Rather, is there not, behind all, some vast average, sufficiently definite, uniform and unswervable Purpose, in the
development of America, (may I not say divine purpose ? only
all is divine purpose,) which pursues its own will, maybe unconscious of itself—of which the puerilities often called history, are
merely crude and temporary emanations, rather than influences
or causes ? and of which the justification is only to be look'd for
in the formulations of centuries to come ? (Let us not be
deceiv'd by flatulent fleeting notorieties, political, official, literary and other. In any profound, philosophical consideration of
our politics, literature, &c., the best-known names of the day
and hitherto—the parties, and their oftenest-named leaders—

the great newspapers and magazines—the authors and artists, and editors—even the Presidents, Congresses, Governors, &c.—are only so many passing spears or patches of grass on which the cow feeds.)

Is there not such a thing as the Philosophy of American History and Politics ? And if so—what is it ?.......Wise men say there are two sets of wills to Nations and to persons—one set that acts and works from explainable motives—from teaching, intelligence, judgment, circumstance, caprice, emulation, greed, &c.—and then another set, perhaps deep, hidden, unsuspected, yet often more potent than the first, refusing to be argued with, rising as it were out of abysses, resistlessly urging on speakers, doers, communities, Nations, unwitting to themselves—the poet to his fieriest words—the Race to pursue its loftiest ideal.......Indeed the paradox of a Nation's life and career, with all its wondrous contradictions, can probably only be explain'd from these two wills, sometimes conflicting, each operating in its sphere, combining in races or in persons, and producing strangest results.

Let us hope there is, (Indeed, can there be any doubt there is ?) this great, unconscious and abysmic second will also, running through the average Nationality and career of America. Let us hope that amid all the dangers and defections of the present, and through all the processes of the conscious will, it alone is the permanent and sovereign force, destined to carry on the New World to fulfil its destinies in the future—to resolutely pursue those destinies, age upon age—to build far, far beyond its past vision, present thought—to form and fashion, and for the general type, Men and Women more noble, more athletic than the world has yet seen—to gradually, firmly blend, from all The States, with all varieties, a friendly, happy, free, religious Nationality—a Nationality not only the richest, most inventive, most productive and materialistic the world has yet known—but compacted indissolubly, and out of whose ample and solid bulk, and giving purpose and finish to it, Conscience, Morals, and all the Spiritual attributes, shall surely rise, like spires above some group of edifices, firm-footed on the earth, yet scaling space and heaven.

No more considering the United States as an incident, or series of incidents, however vast, coming accidentally along the path of Time, and shaped by casual emergencies as they happen to arise, and the mere result of modern improvements, vulgar and lucky, ahead of other nations and times, I would finally plant, as seeds, these thoughts or speculations in the growth of our Republic—that it is the deliberate culmination and result of all the Past—that here too, as in all departments of the Universe, regular laws, (slow and sure in acting, slow and sure in ripening,) have controll'd and govern'd, and will yet control and govern—and that those laws can no more be baffled or steer'd clear of, or vitiated, by chance, or any fortune or opposition, than the laws of winter and summer, or darkness and light.

The old theory of a given country or age, or people, as something isolated and standing by itself—something which only fulfils its luck, eventful or uneventful—or perhaps some meteor, brilliantly flashing on the background or foreground of Time—is indeed no longer advanced among competent minds, as a theory for History—has been supplanted by theories far wider and higher........The development of a Nation—of the American

Republic, for instance, with all its episodes of peace and war—the events of the past, and the facts of the present—aye, the entire political and intellectual processes of our common race—if beheld from a point of view sufficiently comprehensive, would doubtless exhibit the same regularity of order and exactness, and the same plan of cause and effect, as the crops in the ground, or the rising and setting of the stars.

Great as they are, therefore, and greater far to be, the United States too are but a series of steps in the eternal process of creative thought. And here is to my mind their final justification, and certain perpetuity. There is in that sublime process, in the laws of the Universe—and, above all, in the moral law—something that would make unsatisfactory, and even vain and contemptible, all the triumphs of war, the gains of peace, and the proudest worldly grandeur of all the Nations that have ever existed, or that, (ours included,) now exist, except that we constantly see, through all their worldly career, however struggling and blind and lame, attempts, by all ages, all peoples, according to their development, to reach, to press, to progress on, and farther on, to more and more advanced ideals.

The glory of the Republic of The United States, in my opinion, is to be, that, emerging in the light of the Modern and the splendor of Science, and solidly based on the past, it is to cheerfully range itself, and its politics are henceforth to come, under those universal laws, and embody them, and carry them out to serve them.......And as only that individual becomes truly great who understands well that, (while complete in himself in a certain sense,) he is but a part of the divine, eternal scheme, and whose special life and laws are adjusted to move in harmonious relations with the general laws of Nature, and especially with the moral law, the deepest and highest of all, and the last vitality of Man or State—so those Nations, and so the United States, may only become the greatest and the most continuous, by understanding well their harmonious relations with entire Humanity and History, and all their laws and progress, and sublimed with the creative thought of Deity, through all time, past, present and future. Thus will they expand to the amplitude of their destiny, and become splendid illustrations and culminating parts of the Kosmos, and of Civilization.

Are not these—or something like these—the simple, perennial Truths now presented to the Future of the United States, out of all its Past, of war and peace ? Has not the time come for working them in the tissue of the coming History and Politics of The States ? And, (as gold and silver are cast into small coin,) are not, for their elucidation, entirely new classes of men, uncommitted to the past, fusing The Whole Country, adjusted to its conditions, present and to come, imperatively required, Seaboard and Interior, North and South ? and must not such classes begin to arise, and be emblematic of our New Politics and our real Nationality ?

Now, and henceforth, and out of the conditions, the results of the War, of all the experiences of the past—demanding to be rigidly construed with reference to the whole Union, not for a week or year, but immense cycles of time, come crowding and gathering in presence of America, like veil'd giants, original, native, larger questions, possibilities, problems, than ever before. To-day, I say, the evolution of The United States, (South, and Atlantic Seaboard, and especially of the Mississippi

Valley, and the Pacific slope,) coincident with these thoughts and problems, and their own vitality and amplitude, and winding steadily along through the unseen vistas of the future, affords the greatest moral and political work in all the so-far progress of Humanity. And fortunately, to-day, after the experiments and warnings of a hundred years, we can pause and consider and provide for these problems, under more propitious circumstances, and new and native lights, and precious even if costly experiences—with more political and material advantages to illumine and solve them—than were ever hitherto possess'd by a Nation.

Yes : The summing-up of the tremendous moral and military perturbations of 1861–'65, and their results—and indeed of the entire hundred years of the past of our National experiment, from its inchoate movement down to the present day, (1775–1876)—is, that they all now launch The United States fairly forth, consistently with the entirety of Civilization and Humanity, and in main sort the representative of them, leading the van, leading the fleet of the Modern and Democratic, on the seas and voyages of the Future.

And the real History of the United States—starting from that great convulsive struggle for Unity, triumphantly concluded, and *the South* victorious, after all—is only to be written at the remove of hundreds, perhaps a thousand, years hence.

EDITOR'S NOTES

These notes are intended to give the reader a fuller sense of the context of the writing of *Memoranda During the War*, and a clearer view of some of the major persons, places, and events to which Whitman refers, sometimes with the offhand presumption of his readers' familiarity with them. These notes do not attempt, however, to identify or describe in any detail the scores of wounded soldiers Whitman names in the text. To readers interested in a more thorough knowledge of these many men, I strongly commend the "Whitman's Memory" website, compiled with astounding meticulousness by Kenneth M. Price, Martin G. Murray, and Robert K. Nelson, in which the names and biographical essentials of all the soldiers Whitman mentions are catalogued. View the site at: http://jefferson.village.virginia.edu/fdw/volume2/price.

1. What Whitman has in mind when he speaks of "the mushy influences of current times" is of course difficult to specify. But from roughly contemporaneous writing (especially in *Democratic Vistas*) we can be fairly certain that the poet is passing oblique judgment on, not least, the swift ascendancy of immense monied interests, in local and national politics, that would blossom shortly into a whole cultural climate, later to be known as the Gilded Age. The nation's

return to the pettiness and money-getting corruption that Whitman thought had reached as desperate a pitch as it possibly could *before* the war, in the later 1850s, distressed him particularly, especially as this devolution seemed to Whitman to forget and even to rebuke the nobility, self-sacrifice, and heroism he had witnessed in the war.

2. The "large brick mansion" Whitman refers to is the Lacy Mansion, poised on a small hill above the Rappahannock River, and transformed after the Battle of Fredericksburg into a Union field hospital. In one of the war's proliferating ironies, at the Lacy Mansion at the time of Whitman's arrival was also Clarissa Harlowe Barton—better known as Clara Barton, famously dedicated nurse and care-giver to Union troops, and future founder of the American Red Cross. Both Barton and Whitman found around them remnants of the disastrous Battle of Fredericksburg, a demoralizing catastrophe for the soldiers of the Union army, who on December 13, 1862, were killed in massive numbers as they attacked fortified Confederate positions at Marye's Heights. The terrible defeat—the Army of the Potomac lost roughly 12,000 men—returned the Union soldiers to the dismal winter camp at Falmouth, where Whitman finds them, and resulted in Major General Ambrose Burnside's removal from command.

3. Aquia Creek Landing was a major transport depot through which Whitman would pass several times during the war. Railroad tracks led directly north from Fredericksburg to the landing, where one could then take a steamship thirty miles north and east up the Potomac to Washington D.C.

4. By the time of Whitman's arrival, there were roughly three dozen hospitals in the Washington, D.C., area, varying widely in quality and structure of facility. Whitman traveled widely through the sites, which by the summer of 1863, according to Whitman, had multiplied to "some fifty or sixty" camps for the wounded and infirm (see the section "Aug., Sep., and Oct., '63—The Hospitals," p. 45). In *Memoranda* we find him chiefly occupied with the hospitals at Armory Square and Judiciary Square, Campbell, Douglas, Carver, and the Patent Office Hospitals. Curiously, when Whitman returned to Washington in January of 1865, after himself convalescing for some months in Brooklyn, he was employed as a clerk in the Bureau of Indian Affairs; his workplace was the same U.S. Patent Office, where some years earlier he had toured as a friend to the wounded.

5. On October 29, 1864, Whitman published a piece in the *New York Times* entitled, "Fifty-First New York City Veterans." This was his brother George Whitman's regiment, the first with which he came into close contact (at Falmouth, after Fredericksburg, where George, having been wounded in the cheek, was promoted to Captain). As Whitman observed in his article, the regiment fought in an extensive array of battles, from Bull Run and horrifically bloody Antietam to Fredericksburg, the Wilderness, Spotsylvania, and Cold Harbor.

6. The battle Whitman goes on to describe was another disastrous defeat for the Army of the Potomac, and one of Confederate General Robert E. Lee's most brilliant victories. Whitman's account mentions several of the major figures: Major General Joseph Hooker, who had replaced Burnside

as commander of the Army of the Potomac but was routed at Chancellorsville by a force only half the size of his own; Confederate Lieutenant General Thomas J. "Stonewall" Jackson, who launched a brilliant cavalry attack to scatter Hooker's forces, but who was accidentally wounded, mortally, by his own men on the evening of the assault (on May 2, 1863); and Major General John Sedgwick, whose men fought valiantly to come to Hooker's aid, but were by the fourth of May driven back, with Hooker, across the Rappahannock at Fredericksburg.

7. As Whitman indicates, the Battle of Gettysburg was a decisive, crucial victory for the Union, and marked a turning point in the war. Major General George Gordon Meade, who replaced Hooker as commander of the Army of the Potomac, defeated Lee's troops on July 3, 1863, in a battle that culminated in a Confederate charge led by Major General George Pickett against a solid Federal position on Cemetery Ridge. By the time of his retreat, Lee had lost nearly one-third of his army.

8. "Mr. Stanton" is Edwin McMasters Stanton, Lincoln's Secretary of War.

9. At the time of the visit to New York City Whitman recalls in his note (February 18, 1861), Lincoln was president-elect of an already wobbly Union. Only one day earlier, Jefferson Davis had been inaugurated as President—provisionally—of the newly-forming Confederacy. By this time South Carolina, Mississippi, Florida, Alabama, Georgia, Louisiana, and Texas had voted to secede from the Union. When Whitman writes of "anxiety in certain quarters" for Lincoln's safety, he is understating: already fears over the threat of his assassination were quite

reasonably high, and among the Democrats of New York, Lincoln, the Republican, had still more reason to feel ill at ease.

10. "McClellan" is Major General George B. McClellan, commander at one time of all the Union forces, and later of only the Army of the Potomac, until relieved of duty in November of 1862. McClellan had earned the distrust of Republican leadership in Washington for his tactical hesitancy as a commander on the Virginia Peninsula, which some in Washington — particularly Stanton — took to be evidence of timidity, or incompetence, or traitorousness. The popular McClellan would challenge Lincoln for the Presidency in 1864.

11. Culpepper was the site of the winter camp of the Army of the Potomac in 1864. "General S." is Major General William Tecumseh Sherman, who would lead Union forces through much of the near-western theatre of the war, and through the Carolinas.

12. Whitman was first employed in Washington as a clerk in the paymaster's office. His superior was Major Lyman S. Hapgood. The man who got him the job was another clerk in the office and a devoted supporter of Whitman's, Charles W. Eldridge, who had published the 1860 edition of *Leaves of Grass* in Boston.

13. This episode is, chronologically, an oddity. At this point in the text, Whitman has taken us up through the early summer of 1864. But Whitman left Washington on June 23, 1864, and in October of 1864 — if one is following the text chronologically, presumably the date of this entry — Whitman was not on Pennsylvania Avenue but at home in Brooklyn, convalescing from an illness he contracted in Washington (which proved a harbinger of his debilitating stroke of 1873). Consultation with a calendar shows us that *Saturday* October 24 actually

takes place in 1863. Whitman makes the editorial decision to place this and another autumnal episode from 1863 ("A Yankee Soldier") later in the text, we might presume, to contribute to the sense of the book as an ongoing, uninterrupted journal of Washington and its environs. It is one instance in which we can see how Whitman labors to manufacture the effects—of a diarist's offhand immediacy, say—he wishes his *Memoranda* to possess.

14. "Moseby" is Colonel John S. Mosby, one of the best "guerilla" fighters for the Confederacy, whose task it was to raid the Union's supply-lines with enough force and tenacity to insure that a substantial number of Union troops would, of necessity, be pulled back from the front to defend them.

15. This entry marks Whitman's return to Washington from his convalescence in Brooklyn. He arrived back on January 23, 1865.

16. Whitman had reason to be particularly attentive to Southern "escapees," or deserters. His closest companion and most impassioned attachment of this time was Peter Doyle, originally of Limerick, Ireland, who had fought for the Confederates and was wounded in 1862, deserting to the North in 1863, where he was captured by Union soldiers and imprisoned until he pledged not to re-join the Confederacy. Doyle worked as a streetcar operator, which is how, in early 1865, he met Whitman.

17. Buoyed by Major General Philip Sheridan's victories in the Shenandoah Valley, and Sherman's in the South, Lincoln won a substantial victory over George McClellan on November 8, 1864, taking 221 electoral votes to his opponent's 21 (winning the popular vote 2,203,831 to 1,797,019). Lincoln's victory was, among other things, a strong ratifica-

tion of the Union's resolve not to seek a truce with the South, but to continue to fight the war to its end.

18. Despite the rhetorical indications of this episode, Whitman was not present at Lincoln's assassination, but heard of it at his home in Brooklyn (on this, see the end of the later section, "Battle of Bull Run"). Peter Doyle, though, was at Ford's Theatre. Whitman borrowed a great deal from Doyle's first-hand account, and from other sources, incorporating all of this material into the lecture he would give repeatedly in later life, "Death of Abraham Lincoln" (see Appendix 1, p. 144).

19. In the printed editions of *Memoranda*, this word appears as "written." Extant gift copies at the Library of Congress show a pencilled correction, in Whitman's hand, changing "written" to "witless."

20. Whitman's brother George was taken prisoner on September 30, 1864, at the Battle of Poplar Springs Church. Whitman's anger here is directed not only at the South; he was also furious with the Lincoln administration for its part in the breakdown and eventual halt of prisoner exchanges between the Union and the Confederacy. Publicly, Union officials blamed the cessation of prisoner exchanges on the Confederacy, and their obdurate refusal to trade back to the North captured African-American soldiers, whom they considered not prisoners of war but property, taken in hostility and now recovered. In response to this policy, and more directly to the allegations that Confederate Lieutenant General Nathan Bedford Forrest had massacred captured black Federal troops in Tennessee, when he took Fort Pillow in April 1864, the Union suspended prisoner exchanges. This led, inevitably, to horrific overcrowding, and

to the conditions of which Whitman here speaks. In truth, though, the Union logic was less egalitarian than pragmatic: Ulysses S. Grant, now commander of the Army of the Potomac, well knew that the absence of returned troops would hurt the undermanned Confederacy far more drastically than it would the Union. To Whitman's anger and dismay, this logic left thousands of soldiers like George Whitman to their fates. (George would be released on February 22, 1865.)

21. "Calhoun" is Senator John Caldwell Calhoun, from South Carolina, who argued before the war—often in debate with Senator Daniel Webster—for the sovereignty of individual states, and for their sovereign right to nullify Federal legislation and resist Federal incursion.

22. See Whitman's *Democratic Vistas*, as well as the furious polemic of 1856, "The Eighteenth Presidency!" This venomous piece went unpublished as a whole in Whitman's day, but portions of it would be incorporated into "Democratic Vistas," as well as into some of the concluding paragraphs of *Memoranda*.

23. For an earlier version of this fulmination, see Whitman's 1856 essay, "The Eighteenth Presidency!"

24. Whitman here casts a cold eye on Reconstruction (1865–1876), the Republican attempt to reshape the post-war South. Whitman objects to what he sees as the needless humiliation of the South by Reconstruction—though he does not note that the policies of Reconstruction, however flawed or corrupt or mismanaged, also offered African Americans their best prospect for fuller enfranchisement as American citizens. With the eventual collapse of Reconstruction came, too, the foreclosure of much of that promise.

Abraham Lincoln, pictured January 8, 1864.
Taken by the Brady National Photographic Art Gallery of Washington D.C.

APPENDICES

DEATH OF ABRAHAM LINCOLN

Lecture Deliver'd in New York, April 14 1879 —
In Philadelphia, '80 — in Boston, '81

How often since that dark and dripping Saturday—that chilly April day, now fifteen years bygone—my heart has entertain'd the dream, the wish, to give of Abraham Lincoln's death, its own special thought and memorial. Yet now the sought-for opportunity offers, I find my notes incompetent, (why, for truly profound themes, is statement so idle? why does the right phrase never offer?) and the fit tribute I dream'd of, waits unprepared as ever. My talk here indeed is less because of itself or anything in it, and nearly altogether because I feel a desire, apart from any talk, to specify the day, the martyrdom. It is for this, my friends, I have call'd you together. Oft as the rolling years bring back this hour, let it again, however briefly, be dwelt upon. For my own part, I hope and desire, till my own dying day, whenever the 14th or 15th of April comes, to annually gather a few friends, and hold its tragic reminiscence. No narrow or sectional reminiscence. It belongs to these States in their entirety—not the North only, but the South—perhaps belongs most tenderly and devoutly to the South, of all; for there, really, this man's birthstock. There and thence his antecedent stamp. Why should I not say that thence his manliest traits—his universality—his canny, easy ways and words upon the surface—his inflexible determination and courage at heart? Have you never realized it, my friends, that Lincoln, though grafted on the West, is essentially, in personnel and character, a Southern contribution?

And though by no means proposing to resume the Secession war to-night, I would briefly remind you of the public conditions preceding that contest. For twenty years, and especially during the four or five before the war actually began, the aspect of affairs in the United States, though without the flash of military excitement, presents more than the survey of a battle, or any extended campaign, or series, even of Nature's convulsions. The hot passions of the South—the strange mixture at the North of inertia, incredulity, and conscious power—the incendiarism of the abolitionists—the rascality and *grip* of the politicians, unparalle'd in any land, any age. To these I must not omit adding the honesty of the essential bulk of the people everywhere—yet with all the seething fury and contradiction of their natures more arous'd than the Atlantic's waves in wildest equinox. In politics, what can be more ominous, (though generally unappreciated then)—what more significant than the Presidentiads of Fillmore and Buchanan? proving conclusively that the weakness and wickedness of elected rulers are just as likely to afflict us here, as in the countries of the Old World, under their monarchies, emperors, and aristocracies. In that Old World were everywhere heard underground rumblings, that died out, only to again surely return. While in America the volcano, though civic yet, continued to grow more and more convulsive—more and more stormy and threatening.

In the height of all this excitement and chaos, hovering on the

edge at first, and then merged in its very midst, and destined to
play a leading part, appears a strange and awkward figure. I shall
not easily forget the first time I ever saw Abraham Lincoln. It
must have been about the 18th or 19th of February, 1861. It was
rather a pleasant afternoon, in New York city, as he arrived there
from the West, to remain a few hours, and then pass on to Washington, to prepare for his inauguration. I saw him in Broadway,
near the site of the present Post-office. He came down, I think
from Canal street, to stop at the Astor House. The broad spaces,
sidewalks, and street in the neighborhood, and for some distance, were crowded with solid masses of people, many thousands. The omnibuses and other vehicles had all been turn'd off,
leaving an unusual hush in that busy part of the city. Presently
two or three shabby hack barouches made their way with some
difficulty through the crowd, and drew up at the Astor House
entrance. A tall figure step'd out of the centre of these barouches,
paus'd leisurely on the sidewalk, look'd up at the granite walls
and looming architecture of the grand old hotel—then, after a
relieving stretch of arms and legs, turn'd round for over a minute
to slowly and good-humoredly scan the appearance of the vast
and silent crowds. There were no speeches—no compliments—
no welcome—as far as I could hear, not a word said. Still much
anxiety was conceal'd in that quiet. Cautious persons had fear'd
some mark'd insult or indignity to the President-elect—for he
possess'd no personal popularity at all in New York city, and very
little political. But it was evidently tacitly agreed that if the few
political supporters of Mr. Lincoln present would entirely
abstain from any demonstration on their side, the immense
majority, who were any thing but supporters, would abstain on

their side also. The result was a sulky, unbroken silence, such as certainly never before characterized so great a New York crowd.

Almost in the same neighborhood I distinctly remember'd seeing Lafayette on his visit to America in 1825. I had also personally seen and heard, various years afterward, how Andrew Jackson, Clay, Webster, Hungarian Kossuth, Filibuster Walker, the Prince of Wales on his visit, and other celebres, native and foreign, had been welcom'd there—all that indescribable human roar and magnetism, unlike any other sound in the universe—the glad exulting thunder-shouts of countless unloos'd throats of men! But on this occasion, not a voice—not a sound. From the top of an omnibus, (driven up one side, close by, and block'd by the curbstone and the crowds,) I had, I say, a capital view of it all, and especially of Mr. Lincoln, his look and gait—his perfect composure and coolness— his unusual and uncouth height, his dress of complete black, stovepipe hat push'd back on the head, dark-brown complexion, seam'd and wrinkled yet canny-looking face, black, bushy head of hair, disproportionately long neck, and his hands held behind as he stood observing the people. He look'd with curiosity upon that immense sea of faces, and the sea of faces return'd the look with similar curiosity. In both there was a dash of comedy, almost farce, such as Shakspere puts in his blackest tragedies. The crowd that hemm'd around consisted I should think of thirty to forty thousand men, not a single one his personal friend—while I have no doubt, (so frenzied were the ferments of the time,) many an assassin's knife and pistol lurk'd in hip or breast-pocket there, ready, soon as break and riot came.

But no break or riot came. The tall figure gave another relieving stretch or two of arms and legs; then with moderate pace, and accompanied by a few unknown looking persons, ascended the portico-steps of the Astor House, disappear'd through its broad entrance—and the dumb-show ended.

I saw Abraham Lincoln often the four years following that date. He changed rapidly and much during his Presidency—but this scene, and him in it, are indelibly stamped upon my recollection. As I sat on the top of my omnibus, and had a good view of him, the thought, dim and inchoate then, has since come out clear enough, that four sorts of genius, four mighty and primal hands, will be needed to the complete limning of this man's future portrait—the eyes and brains and finger-touch of Plutarch and Eschylus and Michel Angelo, assisted by Rabelais.

And now—(Mr. Lincoln passing on from this scene to Washington, where he was inaugurated, amid armed cavalry, and sharpshooters at every point—the first instance of the kind in our history—and I hope it will be the last)—now the rapid succession of well-known events, (too well known—I believe, these days, we almost hate to hear them mention'd)—the national flag fired on at Sumter—the uprising of the North, in paroxysms of astonishment and rage—the chaos of divided councils—the call for troops—the first Bull Run—the stunning cast-down, shock, and dismay of the North—and so in full flood the Secession war. Four years of lurid, bleeding, murky, murderous war. Who paint those years, with all their scenes?—the hard-fought engagements—the defeats, plans, failures—the gloomy hours, days, when our Nationality seem'd hung in pall of doubt, perhaps death—the Mephistophelean sneers of foreign lands and attachés—the dreaded Scylla of European interference, and the Charybdis of the tremendously dangerous latent strata of secession sympathizers throughout the free States, (far more numerous than is supposed)—the long marches in summer—the hot sweat, and many a sunstroke, as on the rush to Gettysburg in '63—the night battles in the woods, as under Hooker at Chancellorsville—the camps in winter—the military prisons—the hospitals—(alas! alas! the hospitals.)

The Secession war? Nay, let me call it the Union war. Though whatever call'd, it is even yet too near us—too vast and too closely overshadowing—its branches unform'd yet, (but certain,) shooting too far into the future—and the most indicative and mightiest of them yet ungrown. A great literature will yet arise out of the era of those four years, those scenes—era compressing centuries of native passion, first-class pictures, tempests of life and death—an inexhaustible mine for the histories, drama, romance, and even philosophy, of peoples to come—indeed the verteber of poetry and art, (of personal character too,) for all future America—far more grand, in my opinion, to the hands capable of it, than Homer's siege of Troy, or the French wars to Shakspere.

But I must leave these speculations, and come to the theme I have assign'd and limited myself to. Of the actual murder of President Lincoln, though so much has been written, probably the facts are yet very indefinite in most persons' minds. I read from my memoranda, written at the time, and revised frequently and finally since.

The day, April 14, 1865, seems to have been a pleasant one throughout the whole land—the moral atmosphere pleasant too—the long storm, so dark, so fratricidal, full of blood and doubt and gloom, over and ended at last by the sun-rise of such an absolute National victory, and utter break-down of Secessionism—

we almost doubted our own senses! Lee had capitulated beneath the apple-tree of Appomattox. The other armies, the flanges of the revolt, swiftly follow'd. And could it really be, then? Out of all the affairs of this world of woe and failure and disorder, was there really come the confirm'd, unerring sign of plan, like a shaft of pure light—of rightful rule—of God? So the day, as I say, was propitious. Early herbage, early flowers, were out. (I remember where I was stopping at the time, the season being advanced, there were many lilacs in full bloom. By one of those caprices that enter and give tinge to events without being at all a part of them, I find myself always reminded of the great tragedy of that day by the sight and odor of these blossoms. It never fails.)

But I must not dwell on accessories. The deed hastens. The popular afternoon paper of Washington, the little "Evening Star," had spatter'd all over its third page, divided among the advertisements in a sensational manner, in a hundred different places, *The President and his Lady will be at the Theatre this evening....* (Lincoln was fond of the theatre. I have myself seen him there several times. I remember thinking how funny it was that he, in some respects the leading actor in the stormiest drama known to real history's stage through centuries, should sit there and be so completely interested and absorb'd in those human jack-straws, moving about with their silly little gestures, foreign spirit, and flatulent text.)

On this occasion the theatre was crowded, many ladies in rich and gay costumes, officers in their uniforms, many well-known citizens, young folks, the usual clusters of gas-lights, the usual magnetism of so many people, cheerful, with perfumes, music of violins and flutes—(and over all, and saturating all, that vast, vague wonder, *Victory,* the nation's victory, the triumph of the

Union, filling the air, the thought, the sense, with exhilaration more than all music and perfumes.)

The President came betimes, and, with his wife, witness'd the play from the large stage-boxes of the second tier, two thrown into one, and profusely draped with the national flag. The acts and scenes of the piece—one of those singularly written compositions which have at least the merit of giving entire relief to an audience engaged in mental action or business excitements and cares during the day, as it makes not the slightest call on either the moral, emotional, esthetic, or spiritual nature—a piece, ("Our American Cousin,") in which, among other characters, so call'd a Yankee, certainly such a one as was never seen, or the least like it ever seen, in North America, is introduced in England, with a varied fol-de-rol of talk, plot, scenery, and such phantasmagoria as goes to make up a modern popular drama—had progress'd through perhaps a couple of its acts, when in the midst of this comedy, or non-such, or whatever it is to be call'd, and to offset it, or finish it out, as if in Nature's and the great Muse's mockery of those poor mimes, came interpolated that scene, not really or exactly to be described at all, (for on the many hundreds who were there it seems to this hour to have left a passing blur, a dream, a blotch)—and yet partially to be described as I now proceed to give it. There is a scene in the play representing a modern parlor, in which two unprecedented English ladies are inform'd by the impossible Yankee that he is not a man of fortune, and therefore undesirable for marriage-catching purposes; after which, the comments being finish'd, the dramatic trio make exit, leaving the stage clear for a moment. At this period came the murder of Abraham Lincoln. Great as all its manifold train, circling round it, and stretching into the future for many a century, in the politics, history, art, &c., of the New World, in point of fact the main thing, the actual murder, transpired with the quiet and simplicity of any commonest occurrence—the bursting of a bud or pod in the growth of vegetation, for instance. Through the general hum following the stage pause, with the change of positions, came the muffled sound of a pistol-shot, which not one-hundredth part of the audience heard at the time—and yet a moment's hush—somehow, surely, a vague startled thrill—and then, through the ornamented, draperied, starr'd and striped space-way of the President's box, a sudden figure, a man, raises himself with hands and feet, stands a moment on the railing, leaps below to the stage, (a distance of perhaps fourteen or fifteen feet,) falls out of position, catching his boot-heel in the copious drapery, (the American flag,) falls on one knee, quickly recovers himself, rises as if nothing had happen'd, (he really sprains his ankle, but unfelt then)—and so the figure, Booth, the murderer, dress'd in plain black broadcloth, bare-headed, with full, glossy, raven hair, and his eyes like some mad animal's flashing with light and resolution, yet with a certain strange calmness, holds aloft in one hand a large knife—walks along not much back from the footlights—turns fully toward the audience his face of statuesque beauty, lit by those basilisk eyes, flashing with desperation, perhaps insanity—launches out in a firm and steady voice the words *Sic semper tyrannis*—and then walks with neither slow nor very rapid pace diagonally across to the back of the stage, and disappears. (Had not all this terrible scene—making the mimic ones preposterous—had it not all been rehears'd, in blank, by Booth, beforehand?)

A moment's hush—a scream—the cry of *murder*—Mrs. Lincoln leaning out of the box, with ashy cheeks and lips, with involuntary cry, pointing to the retreating figure, *He has kill'd the President.* And still a moment's strange, incredulous suspense—and then the deluge!—then that mixture of horror, noises, uncertainty—(the sound, somewhere back, of a horse's hoofs clattering with speed)—the people burst through chairs and railings, and break them up—there is inextricable confusion and terror—women faint—quite feeble persons fall, and are trampled on—many cries of agony are heard—the broad stage suddenly fills to suffocation with a dense and motley crowd, like some horrible carnival—the audience rush generally upon it, at least the strong men do—the actors and actresses are all there in their play-costumes and painted faces, with mortal fright showing through the rouge—the screams and calls, confused talk—redoubled, trebled—two or three manage to pass up water from the stage to the President's box—others try to clamber up—&c., &c.

In the midst of all this, the soldiers of the President's guard, with others, suddenly drawn to the scene, burst in—(some two hundred altogether)—they storm the house, through all the tiers, especially the upper ones, inflamed with fury, literally charging the audience with fix'd bayonets, muskets and pistols, shouting *Clear out! clear out! you sons of* ——..... Such the wild scene, or a suggestion of it rather, inside the play-house that night.

Outside, too, in the atmosphere of shock and craze, crowds of people, fill'd with frenzy, ready to seize any outlet for it, come near committing murder several times on innocent individuals. One such case was especially exciting. The infuriated crowd, through some chance, got started against one man, either for words he utter'd, or perhaps without any cause at all, and were proceeding at once to actually hang him on a neighboring lamp-post, when he was rescued by a few heroic policemen, who placed him in their midst, and fought their way slowly and amid great peril toward the station house. It was a fitting episode of the whole affair. The crowd rushing and eddying to and fro—the night, the yells, the pale faces, many frighten'd people trying in vain to extricate themselves—the attack'd man, not yet freed from the jaws of death, looking like a corpse—the silent, resolute, half-dozen policemen, with no weapons but their little clubs, yet stern and steady through all those eddying swarms—made a fitting side-scene to the grand tragedy of the murder. They gain'd the station house with the protected man, whom they placed in security for the night, and discharged him in the morning.

And in the midst of that pandemonium, infuriated soldiers, the audience and the crowd, the stage, and all its actors and actresses, its paint-pots, spangles, and gas-lights—the life blood from those veins, the best and sweetest of the land, drips slowly down, and death's ooze already begins its little bubbles on the lips.

Thus the visible incidents and surroundings of Abraham Lincoln's murder, as they really occur'd. Thus ended the attempted secession of these States; thus the four years' war. But the main things come subtly and invisibly afterward, perhaps long afterward—neither military, political, nor (great as those are,) historical. I say, certain secondary and indirect results, out of the tragedy of this death, are, in my opinion, greatest. Not the event

of the murder itself. Not that Mr. Lincoln strings the principal
points and personages of the period, like beads, upon the single
string of his career. Not that his idiosyncrasy, in its sudden
appearance and disappearance, stamps this Republic with a
stamp more mark'd and enduring than any yet given by any one
man—(more even than Washington's;)—but, join'd with these,
the immeasurable value and meaning of that whole tragedy lies,
to me, in senses finally dearest to a nation, (and here all our
own)—the imaginative and artistic senses—the literary and dramatic ones. Not in any common or low meaning of those terms,
but a meaning precious to the race, and to every age. A long and
varied series of contradictory events arrives at last at its highest
poetic, single, central, pictorial denouement. The whole
involved, baffling, multiform whirl of the secession period
comes to a head, and is gather'd in one brief flash of lightning-
illumination—one simple, fierce deed. Its sharp culmination,
and as it were solution, of so many bloody and angry problems,
illustrates those climax-moments on the stage of universal Time,
where the historic Muse at one entrance, and the tragic Muse at
the other, suddenly ringing down the curtain, close an immense
act in the long drama of creative thought, and give it radiation,
tableau, stranger than fiction. Fit radiation—fit close! How the
imagination—how the student loves these things! America, too,
is to have them. For not in all great deaths, nor far or near—not
Cæsar in the Roman senate-house, or Napoleon passing away in
the wild night-storm at St. Helena—not Paleologus, falling, des-
perately fighting, piled over dozens deep with Grecian corpses—
not calm old Socrates, drinking the hemlock—outvies that
terminus of the secession war, in one man's life, here in our

midst, in our own time—that seal of the emancipation of three million slaves—that parturition and delivery of our at last really free Republic, born again, henceforth to commence its career of genuine homogeneous Union, compact, consistent with itself.

Nor will ever future American Patriots and Unionists, indifferently over the whole land, or North or South, find a better moral to their lesson. The final use of the greatest men of a Nation is, after all, not with reference to their deeds in themselves, or their direct bearing on their times or lands. The final use of a heroic-eminent life—especially of a heroic-eminent death—is its indirect filtering into the nation and the race, and to give, often at many removes, but unerringly, age after age, color and fibre to the personalism of the youth and maturity of that age, and of mankind. Then there is a cement to the whole people, subtler, more underlying, than any thing in written constitution, or courts or armies—namely, the cement of a death identified thoroughly with that people, at its head, and for its sake. Strange, (is it not?) that battles, martyrs, agonies, blood, even assassination, should so condense—perhaps only really, lastingly condense—a Nationality.

I repeat it—the grand deaths of the race—the dramatic deaths of every nationality—are its most important inheritance-value—in some respects beyond its literature and art—(as the hero is beyond his finest portrait, and the battle itself beyond its choicest song or epic.) Is not here indeed the point underlying all tragedy? the famous pieces of the Grecian masters—and all masters? Why, if the old Greeks had had this man, what trilogies of plays—what epics—would have been made out of him! How the rhapsodes would have recited him! How quickly that quaint tall form would have enter'd into the region where men vitalize gods, and gods divinify men! But Lincoln, his times, his death—great as any, any age—belong altogether to our own, and are autochthonic. (Sometimes indeed I think our American days, our own stage—the actors we know and have shaken hands, or talk'd with—more fateful than any thing in Eschylus—more heroic than the fighters around Troy—afford kings of men for our Democracy prouder than Agamemnon—models of character cute and hardy as Ulysses—deaths more pitiful than Priam's.)

When, centuries hence, (as it must, in my opinion, be centuries hence before the life of these States, or of Democracy, can be really written and illustrated,) the leading historians and dramatists seek for some personage, some special event, incisive enough to mark with deepest cut, and mnemonize, this turbulent Nineteenth century of ours, (not only these States, but all over the political and social world)—something, perhaps, to close that gorgeous procession of European feudalism, with all its pomp and caste-prejudices, (of whose long train we in America are yet so inextricably the heirs)—something to identify with terrible identification, by far the greatest revolutionary step in the history of the United States, (perhaps the greatest of the world, our century)—the absolute extirpation and erasure of slavery from the States—those historians will seek in vain for any point to serve more thoroughly their purpose, than Abraham Lincoln's death.

Dear to the Muse—thrice dear to Nationality—to the whole human race—precious to this Union—precious to Democracy—unspeakably and forever precious—their first great Martyr Chief.

Vigil Strange I Kept on the Field One Night

VIGIL strange I kept on the field one night;
When you, my son and my comrade dropt at my side that day,
One look I but gave which your dear eyes return'd with a look I
    shall never forget,
One touch of your hand to mine O boy, reach'd up as you lay
    on the ground,
Then onward I sped in the battle, the even-contested battle,
Till late in the night reliev'd to the place at last again I made my
    way,
Found you in death so cold dear comrade, found your body son
    of responding kisses, (never again on earth responding,)
Bared your face in the starlight, curious the scene, cool blew the
    moderate night-wind,
Long there and then in vigil I stood, dimly around me the
    battle-field spreading,
Vigil wondrous and vigil sweet there in the fragrant silent night,
But not a tear fell, not even a long-drawn sigh, long, long I
    gazed,
Then on the earth partially reclining sat by your side leaning my
    chin in my hands,
Passing sweet hours, immortal and mystic hours with you
    dearest comrade—not a tear, not a word,
Vigil of silence, love and death, vigil for you my son and My
    soldier,
As onward silently stars aloft, eastward new ones upward stole,
Vigil final for you brave boy, (I could not save you, swift was
    your death,

I faithfully loved you and cared for you living, I think we shall
surely meet again,)
Till at latest lingering of the night, indeed just as the dawn
appear'd,
My comrade I wrapt in his blanket, envelop'd well his form,
Folded the blanket well, tucking it carefully over head and
carefully under feet,
And there and then and bathed by the rising sun, my son in his
grave, in his rude-dug grave I deposited,
Ending my vigil strange with that, vigil of night and battle-field
dim,
Vigil for boy of responding kisses, (never again on earth
responding,)
Vigil for comrade swiftly slain, vigil I never forget, how as day
brighten'd,
I rose from the chill ground and folded my soldier well in his
blanket,
And buried him where he fell.

Whoever You Are Holding Me Now in Hand

WHOEVER you are holding me now in hand,
Without one thing all will be useless,
I give you fair warning before you attempt me further,
I am not what you supposed, but far different.

Who is he that would become my follower?
Who would sign himself a candidate for my affections?

The way is suspicious, the result uncertain, perhaps destructive,
You would have to give up all else, I alone would expect to be
      your sole and exclusive standard,
Your novitiate would even then be long and exhausting,
The whole past theory of your life and all conformity to the
      lives around you would have to be abandon'd,
Therefore release me now before troubling yourself any further,
      let go your hand from my shoulders,
Put me down and depart on your way.

Or else by stealth in some wood for trial,
Or back of a rock in the open air,
(For in any roof'd room of a house I emerge not, nor in
      company,
And in libraries I lie as one dumb, a gawk, or unborn, or dead,)
But just possibly with you on a high hill, first watching lest any
      person for miles around approach unawares,
Or possibly with you sailing at sea, or on the beach of the sea or
      some quiet island,
Here to put your lips upon mine I permit you,
With the comrade's long-dwelling kiss or the new husband's kiss,
For I am the new husband and I am the comrade.

Or if you will, thrusting me beneath your clothing,
Where I may feel the throbs of your heart or rest upon your hip,
Carry me when you go forth over land or sea;
For thus merely touching you is enough, is best,
And thus touching you would I silently sleep and be carried
      eternally.

But these leaves conning you con at peril,
For these leaves and me you will not understand,
They will elude you at first and still more afterward, I will
      certainly elude you,
Even while you should think you had unquestionably caught
      me, behold!
Already you see I have escaped from you.

For it is not for what I have put into it that I have written this
      book,
Nor is it by reading it you will acquire it,
Nor do those know me best who admire me and vauntingly
      praise me,
Nor will the candidates for my love (unless at most a very few)
      prove victorious,
Nor will my poems do good only, they will do just as much evil,
      perhaps more,
For all is useless without that which you may guess at many
      times and not hit, that which I hinted at;
Therefore release me and depart on your way.

When I Heard at the Close of the Day

WHEN I heard at the close of the day how my name had been
      receiv'd with plaudits in the capitol, still it was not a
      happy night for me that follow'd,
And else when I carous'd, or when my plans were accomplish'd,
      still I was not happy,

But the day when I rose at dawn from the bed of perfect health,
  refresh'd, singing, inhaling the ripe breath of autumn,
When I saw the full moon in the west grow pale and disappear
  in the morning light,
When I wander'd alone over the beach, and undressing bathed,
  laughing with the cool waters, and saw the sun rise,
And when I thought how my dear friend my lover was on his
  way coming, O then I was happy,
O then each breath tasted sweeter, and all that day my food
  nourish'd me more, and the beautiful day pass'd well,
And the next came with equal joy, and with the next at evening,
  came my friend,
And that night while all was still I heard the waters roll slowly
  continually up the shores,
I heard the hissing rustle of the liquid and sands as directed to
  me whispering to congratulate me,
For the one I love most lay sleeping by me under the same
  cover in the cool night,
In the stillness in the autumn moonbeams his face was inclined
  toward me,
And his arm lay lightly around my breast—and that night I was
  happy.

Are You the New Person Drawn toward Me?

ARE you the new person drawn toward me?
To begin with take warning, I am surely far different from what
  you suppose;

Do you suppose you will find in me your ideal?
Do you think it so easy to have me become your lover?
Do you think the friendship of me would be unalloy'd
    satisfaction?
Do you think I am trusty and faithful?
Do you see no further than this façade, this smooth and tolerant
    manner of me?
Do you suppose yourself advancing on real ground toward a
    real heroic man?
Have you no thought O dreamer that it may be all maya, illusion?

City of Orgies

CITY of orgies, walks and joys,
City whom that I have lived and sung in your midst will one
    day make you illustrious,
Not the pageants of you, not your shifting tableaus, your
    spectacles, repay me,
Not the interminable rows of your houses, nor the ships at the
    wharves,
Nor the processions in the streets, nor the bright windows with
    goods in them,
Nor to converse with learn'd persons, or bear my share in the
    soiree or feast;
Not those, but as I pass O Manhattan, your frequent and swift
    flash of eyes offering me love,
Offering response to my own—these repay me,
Lovers, continual lovers, only repay me.

To a Stranger

PASSING stranger! you do not know how longingly I look
    upon you,
You must be he I was seeking, or she I was seeking, (it comes
    to me, as of a dream,)
I have somewhere surely lived a life of joy with you,
All is recall'd as we flit by each other, fluid, affectionate, chaste,
    matured,
You grew up with me, were a boy with me or a girl with me,
I ate with you and slept with you, your body has become not
    yours only nor left my body mine only,
You give me the pleasure of your eyes, face, flesh, as we pass,
    you take of my beard, breast, hands, in return,
I am not to speak to you, I am to think of you when I sit alone
    or wake at night alone,
I am to wait, I do not doubt I am to meet you again,
I am to see to it that I do not lose you.

To Mr. and Mrs. S. B. Haskell

Washington
August 10 1863

Mr and Mrs Haskell,

Dear friends, I thought it would be soothing to you to have a few lines about the last days of your son Erastus Haskell of Company K, 141st New York Volunteers. I write in haste, & nothing of importance—only I thought any thing about Erastus would be welcome. From the time he came to Armory Square Hospital till he died, there was hardly a day but I was with him a portion of the time—if not during the day, then at night. I had no opportunity to do much, or any thing for him, as nothing was needed, only to wait the progress of his malady. I am only a friend, visiting the wounded & sick soldiers, (not connected with any society—or State.) From the first I felt that Erastus was in danger, or at least was much worse than they in the hospital supposed. As he made no complaint, they perhaps [thought him] not very bad—I told the [doctor of the ward] to look him over again—he was a much [sicker boy?] than he supposed, but he took it lightly, said, I know more about these fever cases than you do—the young man looks very sick, but I shall certainly bring him out of it all right. I have no doubt the doctor meant well & did his best—at any rate, about a week or so before Erastus died he got really alarmed & after that he & all the doctors tried to help him, but without avail—Maybe it would not have made any difference any how—I think Erastus was broken down, poor boy, before he came to the hospital here—I believe he came here about July 11th—Somehow I took to him, he was a quiet young man, behaved always correct & decent, said little—I used to sit on the side of his bed—I said once, You don't talk any, Erastus, you leave me to do all the talking—he only answered quietly, I was never much of a talker. The doctor wished every one to cheer him up very lively—I was always pleasant & cheerful with him, but did not feel to be very lively—Only once I tried to tell him some amusing narratives, but after a few moments I stopt, I saw that the effect was not good, & after that I never tried it again—I used to sit by the side of his bed, pretty silent, as that seemed most agreeable to him, & I felt it so too—he was generally opprest for breath, & with the heat, & I would fan him—occasionally he would want a drink—some days he dozed a good deal—sometimes when I would come in, he woke up, & I would lean down & kiss him, he would reach out his hand & pat my hair & beard a little, very friendly, as I sat on the bed & leaned over him.

Much of the time his breathing was hard, his throat worked—they tried to keep him up by giving him stimulants, milk-punch, wine &c—these perhaps affected him, for often his mind wandered somewhat—I would say, Erastus, don't you remember me, dear son?—can't you call me by name?—once he looked at me quite a while when I asked him, & he mentioned over in[audibly?] a name or two (one sounded like [Mr.

Setchell]) & then, as his eyes closed, he said quite slow, as if to himself, I don't remember, I dont remember, I dont—it was quite pitiful—one thing was he could not talk very comfortably at any time, his throat & chest seemed stopped—I have no doubt at all he had some complaint besides the typhoid—In my limited talks with him, he told me about his brothers & sisters by name, & his parents, wished me to write his parents & send them & all his love—I think he told me about his brothers living in different places, one in New York City, if I recollect right— From what he told me, he must have been poorly enough for several months before he came to Armory Sq[uare] Hosp[ital]—the first week in July I think he told me he was miles from White House, on the peninsula—previous to that, for quite a long time, although he kept around, he was not at all well—couldn't do much—was in the band as a fifer I believe— While he lay sick here he had his fife laying on the little stand by his side—he once told me that if he got well he would play me a tune on it—but, he says, I am not much of a player yet.

I was very anxious he should be saved, & so were they all—he was well used by the attendants—poor boy, I can see him as I write—he was tanned & had a fine head of hair, & looked good in the face when he first came, & was in pretty good flesh too— (had his hair cut close about ten or twelve days before he died)—He never complained—but it looked pitiful to see him lying there, with such a look out of his eyes. He had large clear eyes, they seemed to talk better than words—I assure you I was attracted to him much—Many nights I sat in the hospital by his bedside till far in the night—The lights would be put out—yet I would sit there silently, hours, late, perhaps fanning him—he always liked to have me sit there, but never cared to talk—I shall never forget those nights, it was a curious & solemn scene, the sick & wounded lying around in their cots, just visible in the darkness, & this dear young man close at hand lying on what proved to be his death bed—I do not know his past life, but what I do know, & what I saw of him, he was a noble boy—I felt he was one I should get very much attached to. I think you have reason to be proud of such a son, & all his relatives have cause to treasure his memory.

I write you this letter, because I would do something at least in his memory—his fate was a hard one, to die so—He is one of the thousands of our unknown American young men in the ranks about whom there is no record or fame, no fuss made about their dying so unknown, but I find in them the real precious & royal ones of this land, giving themselves up, aye even their young & precious lives, in their country's cause—Poor dear son, though you were not my son, I felt to love you as a son, what short time I saw you sick & dying here—it is as well as it is, perhaps better—for who knows whether he is not better off, that patient & sweet young soul, to go, than we are to stay? So farewell, dear boy—it was my opportunity to be with you in your last rapid days of death—no chance as I have said to do any thing particular, for nothing [could be done—only you did not lay] here & die among strangers without having one at hand who loved you dearly, & to whom you gave your dying kiss—

Mr. and Mrs. Haskell, I have thus written rapidly whatever came up about Erastus, & now must close. Though we are strangers & shall probably never see each other, I send you & all Erastus' brothers and sisters my love—

Walt Whitman

I live when home, in Brooklyn, N Y. (in Portland avenue, 4th door north of Myrtle, my mother's residence.) My address here is care of Major Hapgood, paymaster U S A, cor 15th & F st, Washington D C.

INDEX